many ~~...~~

Oct 6, 2006

Letters from
Boerdonk

By Gary Layne Smith
Artwork by Larry Weston

God bless
Daniel Smith

Best Wishes
Larry Weston

HighPoint
PUBLISHING, INC

Printed and bound in the United Stated of America.

First edition. First printing 2006.

Published and distributed by: HighPoint Publishing, Inc.
                                     141 Loop 64
                                     Suite E
                                     Dripping Springs, Texas 78620
                                     (512) 858-2727

Although the author and the publisher have made every effort to ensure the accuracy and completeness of information contained in this book, we assume no responsibility for errors, inaccuracies, omissions, or any inconsistency herein. Any slights of people, places or organizations are unintentional.

This book is available at quantity discounts for bulk purchases. For information, please call (512) 858-2727 or you can visit our web site at http://www.highpointpublishing.com.

Library of Congress Card Catalog Number (LCCN): 2006930034

International Standard Book Number: ISBN-10 1-933190-10-8
                                          ISBN-13 978-1-933190-10-5

The following trademarks appear throughout this book: Alabama University, Auburn University, Chevy Chase's Christmas Vacation, DieHard, ePHOTO, Gene Autry, Lone Ranger, McDonalds, MIT, Monoply, Oakland A's, Rawlings, Red Sox, Roy Rogers, Sears, Texaco, Texas Rangers, Toys for Tots, Trigger, Wal-Mart, World Series, Yankees.

Editor: Milena Christopher
Design by: Larry Weston and Ryan J. Nayman
Production by: Ryan J. Nayman

Reviews and Comments

I read this book the afternoon after I was diagnosed with cancer. It's one of the most powerful, inspiring and loving books I've ever read!

George Peyton Cole, Jr.
Brigadier General (Retired) U.S. Air Force

• • •

Gary Layne Smith brings smiles, tears, and simple lessons of life to us in stories that we all can relate to. Gary's experiences with our Dutch friends and his life in the military are recorded in easy to understand prose that would be great bedtime stories. We who have served in our Armed Forces understand the essentials that Gary shares--that is, family, friends, sports, life on Earth, life with God--in the "low" times we depend on them, in the "high" times we celebrate them. When you think your life's in a "low", read this book and you'll know a "high" is just around the corner! Down-to-earth, respectful of people, and humorous--a winning combination. What a great gift this book is for family, friends and associates.

Leslie F. Kenne
Lt General (Retired) U.S. Air Force

• • •

Letters from Boerdonk relates with warmth and humor events from the family of an Air Force chaplain to drive home the richness of God's grace.

Dr. Newell Williams
President, Brite Divinity School
Texas Christian University

• • •

The book is really a valentine to every military family who has experienced the stress, the separations, the uncertainty, and the fear that they live with daily as part of military life. It is a heartfelt salute to them and a reminder through "Gary Parables" of the One who walks beside them (and each of us, no matter what life path we choose) every day.

Barbara Tyner, PHR
Purdue Research Foundation
Purdue University

• • •

If you like Jan Karon's "Mitford", you'll love Gary Layne Smith's "Boerdonk"! In this remarkable book Gary Layne Smith captures what is both best and hardest about military service--being sent far from friends and family to places you never thought you wanted to go, and then discovering the unexpected riches God has waiting for you there. Throughout this book Gary's message is clear—"This is what it is all about. Getting folks connected to each other and to God."

Lt. Colonel Karen White,
U.S. Air Force

• • •

Gary Layne Smith has a gift for making people feel they are part of his family by telling them his family's stories. His son Daniel told his class the very first school day here at the International School in The Netherlands "my father tells stories for a living". These are funny stories because Gary is not afraid to criticize himself and he laughs when things don't go his way. A healthy approach to life! While the media informs us about culture clashes around the world, Gary shows us in Letters from Boerdonk *that a meeting of minds is a much better alternative. The letters made me laugh, wonder and think. It is great to see your own Dutch culture through American eyes. I highly recommend this book to all expats living in Holland and to all Dutch people dealing with expats.*

Erika Elkady
Teacher, International Secondary School
Eindhoven, The Netherlands

• • •

Letters from Boerdonk *is a delightful book! It reassures the reader that your life can be educational, exciting, and rewarding no matter where in the world you find yourself when you keep an open heart and an open mind.*

Wren Giesen
89-years young

Letters from Boerdonk is a collection of Gary Layne Smith's personal letters circulated to friends and family while he served as an Air Force chaplain in Boerdonk, The Netherlands. It is a delightful read and gives great insight into family, friends, baseball and the good people of his Boerdonk family. Gary is a great raconteur and ties scripture to daily life in a most ingenious way; he tells personal stories. It will bless your life.

Bert Cobb, M.D.
Otolaryngic allergist
eLectionary Ministry
San Marcos, Texas

●　●　●

The value of relationships permeates this delightful book from beginning to the last word! Gary embraces life and is not a spectator. He fully participates in life and relationships and gently pulls the reader into the very world he loves and describes from within. And he has a gift of gab that is so refreshing! His stories radiate acceptance, connect people and events like glue, and shine with love and hope. With humor, he can even connect different cultures across an ocean. Letters from Boerdonk is a huge celebration of what is, and what can be, here on this small planet.

Lisa Dennis
Full-time mother, CPA

●　●　●

Gary wrote devotionals for our Mature Years magazine in 1993 and 1995. The response to his writings to this day remains the highest positive feedback on record from readers around the country who adored his storytelling reflections! The same joyful storytelling skills appear in Letters from Boerdonk and will hugely please untold numbers of readers around the world!

Marvin W. Cropsey
editor, Mature Years magazine
editor, Leader in Christian Education Ministries magazine
managing editor, The New International Lesson Annual
managing editor, Quadrennial Resources
editor, Adult Study Resources
United Methodist Publishing House

●　●　●

This fascinating book paints a beautiful picture of people in The Netherlands and around the world. Gary Layne Smith loves God, his family, his fellow man, his many close friends, the villagers of Boerdonk with their distinctive customs, the bells of the Boerdonk Catholic Church, sports; particularly baseball. His strong sense of humor, his unique style of writing, his subject matter makes this book a treasure – one you won't want to put down.

Elizabeth Withrow
94-years young retired Science teacher, birder, and columnist
North American Bluebird Society Award, 2006
Limestone County Outstanding Senior Citizen, 2006

● ● ●

Smiles, chuckles, tears - they're all here as you meet these wonderful people. A warm, humorous look at life and our responses to it! I felt wrapped in a comforter of love and laughter as I experienced the book and was sorry it ended.

Judi Faurot
Lecturer (Retired)
University of North Texas

● ● ●

Letters from Boerdonk is about the relationships that provide humor, depth, and meaning to our lives. It is a book written at the intersection where the spiritual, emotional and relational dimensions of our lives meet.

Dr. Michael Young
Minister, District Superintendent (Retired)
Adjunct lecturer, Texas Christian University
United Methodist Church
Central Texas Conference

● ● ●

Letters from Boerdonk is taken from everyday situations of life that teach valuable lessons about the important issues and values of life. These lessons are both simple and profound. Gary Layne Smith has the capacity to write so that both the head and the heart are challenged.

Dr. John Ed Mathison
Senior Minister
Frazer Memorial United Methodist Church
Alabama

● ● ●

I was taken aback by the multiplicity of insights into the lives of several groups. It was also amazing to view the same phenomena through a most unique set of eyes. Insights into the Dutch community culture as seen by a minister, a military man, and a father and husband is truly unique. I doubt that this look at any culture has come from someone wearing these same hats.

Through these visions of life comes a wonderful description of our Lord which would draw many a person into the Church. Yes, the God that I know and worship laughs too. I would bet that anyone who reads the book will have to at least chuckle. The author's son Daniel's description of school life in the Dutch community is unique as he actually lived the experience and it is easy for the reader to see how life at school and home was tightly intertwined. Having lived in a foreign country, I can easily relate to the constant need to learn about the local customs and to adjust your expectations about anything you think you are going to do when you interact with the community.

As I read the book, I could feel the love Gary felt writing it. It would make a wonderful reference for use in a class in political science, history and especially a course in interpersonal relations.

Dr. William Kurtz
Professor Emeritus
Administration and Psychological Services
Texas State University

•   •   •

This book should be rated "E"... E for Everyone and E for Everywhere.

Everyone meaning that is should be read by adults and children; parents in family settings; individuals in quiet times and for encouragement; pastors for instruction; and groups for insight, entertainment, and education.

Everywhere meaning that there should be copies in libraries, at bedsides, in bathrooms, on coffee tables, and beside the most comfortable chair in the house.

Tom Bartels
Frazer Memorial United Methodist Church
Alabama

•   •   •

Witty and disarming, this book leads an unforgettable foray into the heart of "everyman's land", the family. Readers will be captivated by Gary Layne Smith's winsome parabolic style of writing as he shares the interspaces of his own family to forage needed connections between the inside and outside worlds of God's family-at-large. Renowned artist Larry Weston deftly translates the sights, the sounds, and the lessons from other cultures into illustrations that in their own right make this edition of <u>Letters from Boerdonk</u> a collector's item.

Nelwyn B. Moore, Ph.D.
Professor Emerita of Family Science, Texas State University
Marriage and Family Therapist

•　•　•

Thank you so much for giving me the opportunity to read the book. It brings back a lot of memories and reminded us of the warm feelings between your family and ours. You gave us the feeling that you felt it was very nice to be in Boerdonk and being a part of this small town. Maybe that is the reason why you found out during the time that you as a family lived here – that you liked living in a small town, simple with people around who saw that you were interested in them and their small village. Then they opened up to let you into that life and it created friendship and understanding (even without much American words if people did not know each other's language). And it created respect to each other, the less you have around for amusing in the way of stores, noise, traffic, etc...people will go back to where it all starts which is with each other.

Marja Tillaart
Boerdonk, The Netherlands

•　•　•

Acknowledgments

Years ago I used to wonder why authors would write such long Acknowledgment lists at the beginning of a book. Now I understand why. A book is a composition of all the relationships we have in life. These people honored me over the years by allowing me to be their pastor and allowing me into their lives in some way or other.

Pamela my wife, our daughter Amity and son Daniel
They are the joy in life for everyone around them and they granted me permission to tell and write their stories. Amity once told her Auburn classmates that the only stressor she felt in college was "having parents who abandoned me (her) by moving overseas", referring to our getting transferred to the Netherlands after 9/11 in her freshman year at Auburn!

David Sampson
For his comment once that he enjoyed watching me "connect people for eternity." That was fun to hear such a summary. I pray this book continues that practice.

Gladys Ruth Smith Holland my mother
Mom dutifully kept letters of mine on file in her house over the last 35 years. Also thanks to my three brothers David, Rodney and George.

Milena and Ken Christopher
Their belief in me as they asked me to assemble Letters from Boerdonk in book form for HighPoint Publishing Inc. Connecting with the Love of God and with each other is a HighPoint in life, they believe.

Ryan Nayman and Cathy Willhoite
Their technical, professional and pleasant support at HighPoint made even the most tedious aspects of this book enjoyable.

Earlene Inman and Dallas Layne.
Officiating at their marriage ceremony was where I met Milena and Ken.

Norman, Wendy, and Annalaissa Johnson
For the perspective of life's beauty as seen while flying in their Mooney aircraft.

Christ the Redeemer Church in San Marcos, Texas
The members cheered on this book.

Gaye Cobb, Nelwyn Moore, Vicki Barber, Brenda Smith, Peyton Cole, Randy Jacobs, and Erika Elkady.
Greatly appreciated proofing!

Bert Cobb
Incredible insight, engaging conversations, and unwavering belief in this book ministry.

Duane DeWald of Texas A&M University
A lifetime friend and marketing expert.

Michael and Debbie Whittington, Steve and Sharon Berryhill, Lynn Hill, Don and Virginia Timmons, Rodney Coleman, Mark Cusack, Newell Williams, Howard Stone, Mike and Margaret Young, Claudia Thompson, Tom and Nadine Barker, Mae and David Smith, Barbara and Gary Tyner, Karen and Jerry White, Phil and Heather Garrant, Les Katahara, Ron and Lonna Handley, Skip Courter, Tom and Dawn Bush, Roger Carlton, Matt and Carol Jackson, Bill and Natalie Burrell, Scott and Trudy Anderson, Linzy and Brenda Laughhunn, Jolanda Diks, Curtis and Mona Parkerson, Betty Richards, Wren Giesen, Dan and Sue Franks.
What a privilege to be alive on this earth with these jewels.

Larry Weston, artist and illustrator
His talent has greatly enhanced this book and makes one eager to see the next drawing.

All the Dutch people in Boerdonk
They so love life, peace, music, family, and the God who created this all. They taught us the difference between sanely working to "have enough" as opposed to frantically working to "have plenty". They value family life enough to balance work and family.

U.S. Miltary Familes
Thanks to all the incredibly talented, resilient and capable U.S. military men, women, spouses and children who serve our nation through their nomadic lifestyles around the world each day. They pray for peace, I know.

The Holy One
Thanks be to God the Holy One who never gives up on us, never abandons us, and is most interested in connecting all people for all of eternity.

Foreword

Truth.

Contrary to much current thought, it has not disappeared, it is not even completely relative... which is good news for me. I crave truth. Not just the simplistic, garden-variety ability to discern the correct from the false, but a richer, deeper incarnation of truth. Truth that has within it something of goodness, authenticity, clarity and affirmation. <u>Letters from Boerdonk</u> is full to the brim with this "higher calling" of truth.

Now, please do not misunderstand me. Truth cannot be forced or manufactured. Certainly, worthwhile truth cannot be of the "I-told-you-so" variety. And, most certainly, usable truth cannot be of the cheap, heavy-handed "so-the-moral-of-the-story-is" genre. No, truth has to be discovered where it lies. Whether in baseball, bicycles, family relationships or the transient life of military personnel, truth is best observed in its natural habitat.

Gary Layne Smith and Larry Weston understand that. They form a powerful, seamless partnership of words and art that lets you and me find life-affirming, life-impacting truth where it lies.

I have known Gary for more than 30 years. And for 30 years, I have stood shoulder-to-shoulder with Gary observing the events of life. I have been amazed how, time after time, Gary and I can observe the same physical event yet see completely different things. That is the secret - and the magic - of <u>Letters from Boerdonk</u>. This special book allows you and me the opportunity to see for a little while through Gary's eyes. Gary resists the temptation to tell us what to think or how to react. He simply lets us see what he sees: truth where it lies.

Somehow, Larry Weston has acquired (or maybe he had it along - which would make me jealous!) the talent of seeing through the same crystal clear lens that Gary uses. Larry's profound translation of truth into art is mystery I cannot hope to understand, but greatly appreciate.

I have heard that the worst books are a waste, that adequate books are a welcome diversion, but that the best books are a journey. It is into a heavily littered literary landscape that <u>Letters from Boerdonk</u> dares to venture to take us on a long overdue journey. I confessed earlier that I crave truth. But I do not think I am alone. Join me... through this book you now hold in your hand... for an uplifting journey into gentle truth.

Duane A. DeWald
Mays Business School
Texas A&M University

• •

Letters from
Boerdonk

Contents

With Love for Pamela, Amity, and Daniel
To honor Toon and Jacek
In Hope of Peace

Introduction

Letters from Boerdonk

How could a whole book be written about such a small little village?" I was asked by a Dutch woman who lived in the village of Boerdonk (pronounced bor`donk) in southern Netherlands when she heard that I was writing a book about our lives in Boerdonk.

Well, let me tell you a story.

Pam and I met in an Air Force chapel at Edwards Air Force Base in 1972 and we married in that same chapel in 1975 when I was stationed there as a young airman. She was there with her chaplain father and family. Our daughter, Amity, was born in 1981 in Fort Worth, Texas. I graduated from seminary in 1984 and re-entered the Air Force as a chaplain in 1985. Our son Daniel was born in 1989 at what was then the only 'geographically separated unit' (GSU) within the continental United States, Gila Bend Air Force Auxiliary Field, 90 miles south of Phoenix, Arizona and 90 miles from the nearest medical facilities.

Every chaplain, every minister, every soldier, every spouse, every daughter, every son, every family has a story. This book is one chapter of our family's story as told through letters in 2001 and 2002 from the Netherlands, immediately after the 9/11 attacks.

This story is really about the wonderful Dutch people. They welcomed us as Americans into their idyllic life in a little Dutch village in southern Netherlands (Holland). We lived first person with the villagers, experiencing their own hope for peace in a docile land where schools still teach of vivid recollections of World War II and NATO to its children with purpose. Our family was slowly enchanted and affected and changed by the gentle bumping together of American culture and Dutch culture as our family

Pam with some of our friends and neighbors at Boerdonk

sought to embrace their ways, and they sought to introduce us to their ways.

It is also a story of how our family dealt with being separated by an ocean at a time when we would have preferred to have been together. Our prayers were with all the men and women in the U.S. military who had severe situations to deal with, were in war zones, and faced long periods of separation. We learned that even in a beautiful land like Holland you still miss family.

September 2001

We were stationed at Keesler Air Force Base in Mississippi in 2001, our daughter Amity was now a War Eagle at Auburn University in Alabama, and we were fighting the no-see-'em bugs along the muggy Gulf Coast.

When the terrorist airplanes hit the Twin Towers and shocked our nation on 9/11, our Amity called us immediately from Auburn and asked "Daddy, are we at war?" I assured her the world was going to be alright.

Toon & Annie v.d. Tillaart celebrating their 50th wedding anniversary

I soon received military orders to transfer to northern Europe to establish religious services as a chaplain to U.S. military personnel at remote sites in three countries – the Netherlands, northern Germany, and Belgium. We would "live on the economy" which means there is no U.S. military base nor is there U.S. housing. We would find a Dutch home and live among the Dutch.

My wife Pam (left) with friend Marja and daughter Eefie.

In October 2001 our household goods were shipped to the Netherlands and we followed our stuff in November. We had heard of a potential house owned by a Dutch couple named Toon and Annie Tillaart in some village named Boerdonk. But they wanted to interview us first prior to renting, so we were uncertain about whether

3

or not we would get the Boerdonk house. Thanksgiving and Christmas in transition made those days very different. It was the most difficult day of our marriage to say good-by to our daughter Amity at the Atlanta airport on November 14, 2001. I was not sure where the world was heading.

Our daughter Amity (center) with friends Ricky and Lindsay

I had been warned by some senior military officers to not take my family to Europe at this point in time following 9/11. I was told terrorism makes it appear too dangerous to take a family. My wife Pamela (Franks) grew up in a military family as the daughter of a chaplain. She was a Texan also, which helped. She possesses a very strong constitution. She would have nothing to do with staying behind. She never blinked. "I am going with you and we are taking Daniel."

Pam never blinked.

We had no idea that the little Dutch village named Boerdonk would welcome us as a family and allow us to discover it and its wonderful people and its soothing church bells.

This is our local mobile grocery store that rolled into town twice a week.

4

Since we were "in transition" during the Thanksgiving and Christmas season and sent out no Christmas cards or annual Family Christmas letter, we finally wrote an email to bring our families and friends up to date. The first letter was written on Friday March 1, 2002

The first letter is one sent to family and friends back home... a long-overdue letter sent three months after we arrived. Most of the rest of the letters in this book were sermons, which in reality are lessons in life that were given

Our son Daniel in the back of our Boerdonk home

to military personnel in Northern Europe that were sent out weekly as letters to family and friends around the world. The parables told by Jesus were stories that were told about the daily lives of people to illustrate a point about the way God works all around us daily and, at times, quietly. I have taken this approach in my own ministry which should be evident in these letters that you are about to read. Many of the letters describe the wonderful and peaceful people and life in the Dutch village of Boerdonk. These villagers so embraced and welcomed our family and I hope you are able to feel embraced as you read this book also. These letters were our way of trying to describe the village life, the people, their hopes in life, and the weekly lessons learned from the Dutch village of Boerdonk.

Some weeks I would not mail out a lesson from Boerdonk for that week and some person whom I had not met but who had received the weekly stories would email and say, "Hey, what happened in Boerdonk this past week?" People were turning on their computers on Monday morning and wanting to read their weekly dose of Boerdonk happenings!

Thank you for reading these letters. I hope you laugh as you read these. I laughed as I wrote them. I hope you cry sometimes. I did while penning them, delivering them, and sending them. I hope you pray for world peace without ceasing. I do. Our family hopes these letters nudge many toward family harmony, closer community, laughter, and a sense of hopefulness – as the Dutch nudged our family toward such while we were living in one of their villages as the lone American family. The village welcomed us, surrounded us with their stories and ways, and we came back to America much richer in spirit and hope.

Enjoy!

A comment about the church bells notations.

While in Boerdonk it became a habit to write my sermons early each Sunday just as the morning rays began to fill the sky. The quietness and solitude were only broken by the ringing of soothing church bells. What a perfect setting for inspiration and writing. The sound of these bells became a golden thread for me that seemed to link one sermon and letter to another regardless of the subject for that week. With this in mind, I have taken the liberty of adding a brief comment regarding the ringing of the bells before each letter in this book as the bells became an important part of my life and that of my family. The best lessons come directly from life, and I enjoy capturing glimpses of these fleeting moments in real-life stories. Many of these bell reflections still waltz through my head....

First Letter from Boerdonk

March 1, 2002

*Hi from the land of windmills, wooden shoes,
canals, church bells, and little villages.*

We live 90 miles south of Amsterdam in southern Netherlands in a small village called Boerdonk. The 90-mile-drive can take hours due to the traffic congestion, so the best way to get to Amsterdam is by train. Amsterdam and the hamlet we live in are two very different worlds. Amsterdam is full of life and Boerdonk is very quiet and surrounded by farms.

We are getting settled in. We said good-bye to Amity (staying at Auburn) at the Atlanta airport November 14th and arrived in country the 15th. Looked for a house for two weeks, decided on one in a village called Boerdonk. Americans warned us to not live in Boerdonk because "there is nothing there." Signed lease on the 28th of November (most U.S. military families have to spend 4-6 months in a hotel room here... housing is hard to find on the economy and there is no U.S. base nor U.S. military housing), moved

9

"loaner furniture" into the house on December 18th, Amity arrived the 19th, we picked up our car in Germany on the 20th, Christmas came on the 25th, our furniture and our Christmas decorations arrived on January 2nd, Amity set up her room on the 3rd so it would be here for her future visits, she left on the 4th of January, our computer which was damaged in the move got repaired on the 5th of February, our internet service was hooked up on the 7th of February... and we are beginning to feel a bit more connected to the world again. We would prefer to NEVER again move during the holidays. Amity being here over Christmas break made our Christmas, needless to say!

We are renting a wonderful old Dutch house built in 1916 in this very quaint farming village about 20 minutes from the Dutch Air Force base where my office is located. The village is about the size of a neighborhood we lived in while stationed in Alabama – about 150 houses. We look out our windows across the street at the one village church (beautiful Catholic church with bell that rings on the hour), the one village school where all 120 village children attend, the village cemetery, the village bike shop (seems every Dutch citizen owns and rides a bike), and the village dance hall owned by our 76-year-old landlord Toon. By Dutch standards, our house is quite large. Most Americans end up in very small houses. We are fortunate to have a four-bedroom, two-story, two-kitchen Dutch house. The house sits right on the village road like most of the houses in the village. The village is called Boerdonk (Boer means "farm" and donk is elevated land, a place of high ground to build a village in order to stay dry during times of flooding) and is surrounded by milk-producing dairy farms and farming fields. One of Holland's quaint canals runs near the village. About 20 miles from us is where dozens of pig farms are located. Several American families rent houses located ON the pig farms where the houses are attached to the pig barns. Our house was originally a farmhouse and the cow stalls/barn attached to our house has been converted into a nice enclosed storage room for all of our stuff we don't want in the house. We stored some household items in Mississippi anticipating getting a small Dutch house. But we ended up with lots of space and lots of nice storage. We have a huge living/dining room combination, four bedrooms, laundry room, two baths, and a very nice sunroom off the back of the house.

The three problems Americans face with housing over here are 1) availability 2) heating systems 3) landlord relationships (which can be bad). We have been blessed with a wonderful house with a modern heating system and a landlord who can not do enough for us. I think he really likes Pam! Anything that goes wrong with the house he has fixed THAT day. We had a leaky faucet and he replaced ALL the plumbing fixtures in the house the next day. All new faucets in both kitchens and bathrooms, for example. We pay him good rent, and he really likes Pam's smile and loves to serve soft drinks to Daniel.

Remember the TV show Northern Exposure? People in that show WERE the entertainment in the little Alaskan village. Same here in Boerdonk. We are the only Americans in the village. They know what we do all the time. Nothing goes unnoticed. Our landlord (who speaks but a little English) told Pam one time that he knew Pam goes to bed at 10:00 p.m. each night because that is when her sleeping room lights go out. He told her that he knew that Amity stayed up until 1:00 a.m. watching TV when she visited here because "the living room lights stayed on until 1:00 a.m." We had tea with a villager last week (first time in a villager's house), and the next day our landlord told us he knew we had tea at the villager's house.

It is unbelievably quiet in our village. To find a place in Holland so quiet is almost impossible, we have heard, because Holland (actually called The Netherlands) is the second most densely populated country in the world. It is packed with towns and cities. Most Americans tell us they don't know how we live in Boerdonk because it is TOO quiet looking and has no stores, no restaurants, no traffic, and no life. THAT is why we like it. It is very peaceful with no crime.

All 120 village children attend the Boerdonk school which is right across the street from our house and nestled between the church and the village "drinks-only" café. They walk or ride their bikes to school, go home for a 90-minute lunch, and go back to school. Nothing like this in America as far as I know.

Town growth is controlled. Only two houses per year are allowed to be built. And those two houses have to conform to the standard set by the FIRST house built on a street. For instance, if the first house built on a street is a one-story house, then ALL future houses on the street have to be one-story. One man in town has been saving money to build a two-story house on property he has owned for years. But he waited too long and another person built a one-story house first and now all houses on that street have to be one story and no two-story houses are allowed on that street. Conformity is the Dutch way of life.

Daniel gets on a contract Dutch bus each morning at 7:30 a.m. and rides 40 minutes to the village of Volkel to attend an american Department of Defense Dependent School (DoDDS). 70 students, first through sixth grade. All Americans. Kids have to bring their lunch since there is no school lunch system in place in Holland due to the tradition and culture. The students are children of the 130 U.S. military families assigned to the Dutch Air Force base at Volkel. This school only goes through sixth grade, so next year (7th grade for him) he will attend the International Secondary School of Eindhoven (ISSE) at a city called Eindhoven which is about a one-hour bus ride away. The school follows the curriculum of the International Baccalaureate Organization (IBO). That school is going to be quite a culture shock. It is run like a university He will have "courses" like at college. He will have to take Dutch, Spanish, French, and English next year in addition to nine other courses (classes). European kids finish "high school" by age 16, have many more freedoms at a younger age than American parents are accustomed to giving (like young teens traveling alone on the public transportation system). Daniel's current school tries to prepare the kids for next year, so this mid-year switch has been QUITE the shock for Daniel and us. He is strong and has risen to the occasion and has made the adjustment. He takes Dutch and is doing very well with the language. The Boerdonk village kids have become friends of his, and he is learning much Dutch from them. They have to take English in school, so he helps them and they help him.

We take a tour of the International School in Eindhoven next week to see if we are ready for this. We don't have any viable options, so we hope for a positive impression next week.

The Dutch kids color their hair, so Daniel has some red coloring in his flattop. He actually looks good. We noticed that as he changes the color of his hair then our hair changes color also... to grey.

Pam is not teaching. It is a good thing because she has her hands full with getting the house set up, keeping up with Daniel's school demands, and "registering" here in Holland. Like many other European countries, one has to register many things just to live temporarily in the country. We are still in the process of registering utilities, bank accounts, Dutch ID cards for Pam and Daniel, cars, registering with a Dutch doctor. You can not see a doctor until you have registered with one in the nearest town that has a doctor. Boerdonk is too small to have a doctor.

The nearest U.S. commissary for groceries is 90 minutes away at an Army base in Germany. It is small but adequate. The nearest U.S. medical facilities (for Daniel's orthodontist work) are at Bitburg, Germany, which is 3 hours away. We go there monthly for the orthodontic work and while there we stock up on groceries, packing the car full of favorite American items. We take a cooler and get frozen meat, etc.

Twice a week a Dutch grocery truck stops on each street in our village. Fresh fruits, vegetables, milk, and eggs are all stocked in that truck. So that is really nice. Plus they tend to have some tasty chocolates.

Pam is considering applying for a position of Coordinator for the College of Chicago here in this part of Europe. Very few American military spouses can find work in Holland (huge morale issue for younger U.S. military families).

She is going with a group of 11 women on a 4-day trip next month to Poland and the Czech Republic. This would be a "power shopping trip" for women only to buy pottery, woven baskets, etc. Drive all night, shop all day and night and the next day, and return back the next night. Some refer to this trip as the "estrogen express."

It is snowing, hailing, and raining with high winds today, much like all other days this winter. That is the beauty of living in northern Europe up against the North Sea. The grocer (in the truck) named Sander is a nice, polite and helpful young man who speaks very good English and has helped us interpret food labels, bills (we can't tell if our Dutch mail is a bill or an advertisement!), etc. I told him today, "This is bad weather." He said, "Ah, it is not so good weather. This is real Dutch weather." Boy is he right. It ALWAYS rains, drizzles, and is cloudy. At least it has been this way since we arrived in late November.

My job is very different. I was sent here to establish religious worship services and ministerial coverage for U.S. military personnel at six remote "geographically separated units" (GSUs) in northern Germany, Netherlands, and Belgium. Three of them are large enough to warrant weekly Protestant worship services. (My job is to start and conduct these services now that they have a chaplain in the "neighborhood.") None of the sites are U.S. bases. They each exist on foreign bases with U.S. military stationed on the base. So all U.S. military attached are on their own for housing, medical, groceries, etc. For even the most senior officers, finding housing and medical coverage has been challenging. Plus children have to ride for sometimes two hours one way on buses to and from school. Most folks are VERY glad to have a chaplain assigned in the area.

Each Sunday Pam and I drive to Kalkar, Germany to a NATO site to conduct a worship service. It is a one-hour drive. About 30 U.S. NATO families are stationed at Kalkar, mostly officers and some enlisted soldiers. They are so appreciative to have a chaplain there weekly now. The U.S. general at Kalkar was instrumental in pushing hard to get a chaplain over there to these folks. The worship service is held in an abandoned school building which is left over from the Cold War days when U.S. presence here was much greater. Not an ideal worship situation but the people have done a good job of making things work with what they have and creating a "holy place" with small altar and covered windows (terrorism target is of great concern here because the school is unprotected and not on U.S. property). About 40 to 50 men, women, and children attend this worship service.

After this service in Germany, Pam and I drive back home one hour, pick up Daniel, and drive to Volkel, Holland to hold a 6 p.m. worship service for the 130 U.S. military personnel and their families assigned in the area. As in Germany at Kalkar, we have no chapel. At Volkel we set up a make-shift chapel in an old Dutch office building in the conference room. About 40 Americans and Dutch civilians gather for worship here on Sunday evenings. There is some "competition" between the U.S. remote military sites; so right now the competition is benefiting the new chaplain as they each try to accommodate at a level greater than the other site.

The third major site is in Belgium. Right now I have a contract minister doing that weekly service. Funding is a question there. Plus Belgium is seemingly making it more difficult for foreign missionaries to function within the country as all the post-cold war missionary efforts in Europe and Russia have grown to an irritating level, at least to some Europeans. I am going to visit the Belgium site this Thursday and take Pam with me. It is about a two-hour drive one way from our house.

I hope to establish more community by bringing the Christian communities (Catholic and Protestant) at the three sites together for worship and other functions periodically.

We selected to live in this village called Boerdonk as it is most central to the three major sites in Germany, the Netherlands, and Belgium.

The Air Force has not produced the lease car and the cell phone that was supposed to "be waiting for you when you get off the plane." The U.S.A.F. chapel world and the contract world in Germany are supposedly handling this arrangement... this could take a while. I am traveling in my own car at my own expense to these sites at this time.

We took Amity and Daniel on a train ride to Amsterdam on New Year's Eve. We visited the Anne Frank house in Amsterdam plus really enjoyed the two-hour train ride through Holland. Amity will come back in June for a few weeks. I think a couple of her former high school classmates from Boston (Ricky Harrington and his sister Lindsay) are going to come with her this summer. That will be fun. She will spend the rest of the summer working in Boston.

As difficult as it is to be so far from Amity in light of the world situation, I think she is enjoying telling her Auburn friends that she goes to Europe for her college breaks... while they go to Huntsville or Mobile for their breaks!

It is Saturday in Boerdonk and there is not much else to do other than type this long email as a belated Christmas letter to bring you up to date. Sorry about the long note, but now you have heard a bit about Holland.

Love from the Gila Bend of Europe called Boerdonk!
Gary and Pam

Baseball and Brugge

April 14, 2002

*We drove by the ringing church bells as we departed
Boerdonk, heading to visit Brugge yesterday.*

Four long, cold, dreary, wet, quiet months of winter here in Boerdonk have passed for us. Some weekends only the sounds of the church bells punctuate the eerie quietness and cold in this little village near the North Sea of Europe. Our house has been warm and our lives quiet. Too quiet.

I call Boerdonk "Lent personified." It is as if we took a vow of silence when we moved here. The village looks like a ghost town all winter. The only hint that there was life in the village was the smoke curling out of the tops of the chimneys, which we could see as we peered out our windows, hoping for some connection with life.

Kind of quiet in Boerdonk this weekend. It is that way most every weekend. The church bells interrupt the quiet and solitude each hour. So we ventured out to Belgium yesterday.

One family member back in the United States said that if he could only visit one city in Europe on a trip it would be Brugge.

So we left Boerdonk for a day and went to Brugge, Belgium yesterday. Brugge is a medieval city in Belgium known for its lace, chocolate shops, bakeries, and for having the only Michelangelo statue outside of Italy – the Madonna and Child – sitting in the village cathedral. You feel like you step back in time 1,000 years when in Brugge.

Several U.S. families from Volkel piled onto the bus and headed toward the bakeries and the chocolate shops. The women shopped lace stores while we guys pillaged bakery after bakery, chocolate shop after chocolate shop. We even found and ate Belgium waffles hot off the iron... with chocolate topping.

The Kitchins -- Shawn, Pam, Rachael, Kayla, Nolan -- and the Millers -- Jeanne and David and Sarah -- were all there.

Heaven on earth. For a whole day.

On our way back to the bus at the end of the day, Pam dragged us into one last bakery. She pointed to some bread that had apple, cinnamon, and raisins in it and ordered. Shawn thought she ordered a slice of bread... she had ordered the whole loaf. Long three-hour bus trip home, after all. Shawn followed her all the way to the bus. By the time he sat down, he had half the loaf from her. I told him to not even bother trying to get any food from me... I had two croissants. With chocolate filling AND chocolate topping.

I got thirsty and ran out of water. I asked Jeanne Miller if she had any extra water. She was tight but negotiable. I showed her my croissant with chocolate dripping off it and she asked "How much water do you want?" I politely asked her if she wanted a bite of my croissant or if she wanted the whole thing. Wrong question. She took the whole thing. As we all broke bread and drank water there on the bus, she told us she could tell there was a minister around because of the way we talked of food.

Brugge. Chocolate croissants. New friends. Heaven.

We wished Amity were here with us. She would love the lace, the chocolate croissants, the bakeries, and the laughter. We missed her and wished she could be eating with us. It was not our plan to be so far from her.

But our winter days in Boerdonk were beginning to be more bearable. A neighbor in Boerdonk had actually invited us to their home recently for coffee and tea. We were so excited to be asked inside a Dutch home for a chance to actually chat and visit for a little while. Eating with new friends can sustain you on long, cold, wintry, windy nights up against the North Sea. Daniel had insisted on boarding a bus with other village kids and riding to another village for a dance during this "Carnival Time" – a time prior to Lent when parties occur often for adults and kids. We were so glad to see some life in the village at this Carnival Time… after a long winter of seemingly no life in the village except the sounds of the church bells which let us know we were at least still alive.

Kids wore funny costumes and had many colors in their hair. So did some adults. Quite the sight to see. Carnival Time is apparently a sign that spring is approaching.

The house we had tea in was a house that was beautiful in its simplicity. The Dutch decorate nicely without clutter. This family had rented another house for 15 years in the village of Boerdonk. They were not natives of the area and therefore did not have any relatives in the village. They had waited and rented for 15 years in order to be able to finally get approval to build a house.

There is a Friend who sticks closer than a brother. I love the Church because of so many good friends that God has blessed us with through our journey together. Good friends who stick with you through your winter days and your summer days.

The huge cathedral in Brugge stands so high above everything else in the city that it draws people's attention to it. It draws people together just by its sheer magnitude of beauty and awe.

God's love does the same. Draws us together as we marvel at the beauty of Love and Patience in our lives.

Michelangelo's Madonna and Child are in Brugge because at one time the Church in Italy was embarrassed by how human Jesus appeared in the now famous sculpture. Too human was the Christ Child.

As we were standing there studying the Madonna sculpture, Shawn Kitchin whispered to me, "Keep preachin' baseball like you have the last few Sundays. My wife now thinks baseball is holy since you preach about it. Now she is watching baseball on TV with me. I even came home one day, and she had the Cubs on TV. Keep preachin' baseball."

That is my job... to bring families and friends closer together. If God can bring a family closer together through baseball, who am I to not keep preachin' baseball? Such a human thing, this American baseball.

It all hangs together. Life, the church, Boerdonk and its church bells, our humanity, bread, croissants dripping with chocolate, Madonna and Child.

When we returned to Boerdonk, we heard the church bells and they actually sounded good for the first time. We are finding out that we are beginning to get accustomed to the sound of the church bells. They sounded good and were becoming part of our lives. As if we were becoming a part of the life there in Boerdonk.

The church bells remind you that you are not alone in Boerdonk. And I think that IS the reason for church bells

The Car Battery

May 5, 2002

*Throughout the winter the Boerdonk bells rang
every hour, reminding us we are not alone. We
are getting accustomed to the cadence in
our lives established by the bells.*

Two years ago, we were stuck in life, as we all are stuck in life at times. Our life is just like yours. I was #1 on the overseas list and our daughter was nearing the end of high school. We had tried to work it out so as not to be going overseas while she was in high school or college but we failed. With college costs facing us, it was not the time to eject out of the military, nor did we want to be oceans away from Amity as she started college.

We have plans, and sometimes God has other plans.

We tried to hedge our bets. Anticipating not being able to remain close to Amity for her college days, we splurged and gave her a new Dodge Neon for her 18th birthday. She earned it, in our minds. She was shocked beyond description. We tricked her into going with us

21

to her favorite restaurant for a "quiet" dinner... she did not want a party, she said. She was still a bit sad over having to leave Montgomery during her high school days when we were transferred to Hanscom Air Force Base near Boston her sophomore year in high school. She simply wanted a quiet birthday party.

The 30 or 35 folks from her high school and from the chapel shocked her by yelling "Surprise!" in the restaurant when she walked into the room. She opened gifts and our gift was a big box. She opened our big box only to find a series of smaller boxes... she opened several boxes until getting to the key. She thought it was simply a nice, new key to the old car we let her drive. Her friends finally blurted it out... dragging her to the parking lot.

We had hidden the car behind the restaurant and wrapped a big Auburn bow around it... she was going to Auburn after graduation

I love being a parent.

As Tom Bartels said to me, "If she had been a guy, you would have just let her drive and learn how to maintain an old clunker during college. But having a daughter is another matter." He was so right.

We did not want her breaking down at midnight in some old car while we were in some other part of the world, unable to reach and help her. She would never have to open the hood on this Neon.

She treasures that car. And we could move over here knowing we had purchased an insurance policy on the new car... full roadside service, etc. Brand new car.

The restaurant where we surprised her is called the Hartwell House. Very elegant 5-star restaurant outside of Boston in Lexington where Amity worked as a hostess throughout high school. She is majoring in Hotel and Restaurant Management because of falling in love with the profession through her days at the Hartwell House.

She has planned what she calls the "trip of her life" this month en route to coming here to Holland for three weeks. She and a couple of Auburn classmates are going to drive her now 2-year-old Neon to Washington D.C., then to New York City for a few days, and then to Boston for a three-game series between the Yankees and the Red Sox before flying over here for three weeks. Then she will fly back to Boston and work at the Hartwell House for the summer... to make money to put gas into the Neon.

She asked me if there was anything she needed to do to the Neon to get it ready for the trip. She asked me that question months ago. She plans well and usually does what I suggest. I told her she should get a new battery... just to be sure. About $100 dollars at Sears. DieHard. Big one.

We sent her the money and she kept not doing it. That was uncharacteristic for her. Finally last week I put the pressure on. I told her I did not want her driving to D.C. and on to Boston without a new battery. Just to be safe.

She then blurted it out. She told me all her college guy friends laughed at her and said she did not need a new one... said they go years without replacing one. I got frustrated with that young cocky college approach. I told her, "Amity, I do NOT care what your Auburn boy friends think... get a battery." A few days later I called her back... still no battery. Again I heard about the unwanted opinion of the Auburn boys. I told her, "Well, then, you tell those Auburn boys to give you their phone numbers and when your battery is dead in New York at midnight you will call them collect and tell them to come and get you."

Those are the same boys who take her off-road mudding just to get stuck... and to see if they can bury themselves so deep in the mud they have to be towed out.

There. Made myself clear. I went on and told her they were just Alabama boys who LOVE to have their cars break down JUST so they CAN fix them. She laughed and said she knew it... but they have her convinced they are right.

I told her to go to Sears this week and get a new one.

She then said, "Grandma Ruth (my mother in Ohio) laughed and said I don't need a new one. She said the car is only two years old." I told her, "You do not live in Ohio... Ohioans drive their cars until the battery goes dead and leaves them stranded... THEN they get a new one. I know... I AM an Ohioan!"

Then she pulled out the stinger. She said "Uncle Rodney (my brother) even laughed at all this. (He is a truck mechanic... best in the business). He told Grandma Ruth that maybe Gary thinks the car has been recalled or something."

I had had enough. Auburn boys, my mom, and now my own brother all involved. What is the WHOLE world doing involved in this little issue???????

I got off the phone and called my mother. I was sweet for the first part of the phone call.

Then I politely asked, "Mom, may I ask what in the world you and Rodney are doing sticking your noses into my and Amity's business and telling her she does not need a car battery when I have told her to get one? Can you tell me WHY you all are involved????"

She said, "Car BATTERY?"

I said, "Yes, that is what all this is about. I told her she needs to get a new battery, and the whole world is telling her she does not need a new battery. A darn $100 Sears DieHard car battery. I want to know what you think you are doing."

She said, "BATTERY? Amity told me you wanted her to replace the MOTOR in her new Neon. I called Rod about it 'cause Amity was so confused as to why you wanted her to replace the motor. We could not figure it out either."

I could not stop laughing. Battery... motor. Amity and I mixed up two little words.

Called Amity back and did not want to make her feel bad. Told her that now I know why everyone told her to not listen to me... she thought I said to replace the motor. She said, "Battery... motor... what difference does it make?" I said, "What DIFFERENCE does it make????? About $4,900 worth of difference... a motor will cost you $5,000 and a battery only $100. That is why those Alabama boys could drive 10 years without replacing one... motor that is!" JUST like they told her. She could not stop laughing either... right in the middle of finals there at Auburn.

She told me Mom and Rod laughed so hard at me to her about the notion of her needing a new motor that she felt badly for me... she did not want the whole world laughing at her daddy, but she did not want to put her car in the shop for a month to have the motor replaced.

Her friend's car HAS been in the shop for over a month, waiting on a new motor.

I asked her if I could tell you all this story this Sunday... that I did not want to embarrass her by telling the story. She said, "Daddy, it won't embarrass me. You are the one who told me I needed a new motor."

I told her not to even worry about getting a new battery anymore. If the battery goes dead, just call the 1-800 number for Dodge road side warranty... I pay for the coverage every month anyway.

She ended the conversation by saying, "Thanks for the laugh. I needed it. Back to studying for finals. I love you, Daddy."

(She made the trip with no car troubles!)

High/Low

May 12, 2002

Our mornings in Boerdonk begin now with our looking out the kitchen window to gaze at the church steeple as the bells ring. It is a peaceful view and a calming sound.

One American family invited us to their house for dinner a few weeks ago. While eating dinner, one of their children said, "High/Low!" I did not know if I was supposed to duck to avoid some high flying object or lift my feet up so as to avoid some object scooting across the floor! I just stayed quiet and kept eating, waiting to see what I was supposed to do next. Then one child eagerly started with "Well, my low for the day was... " and ended with "my high for the day was... " They have a family tradition - each night at dinner each person gives their "high" and their "low" for the day. I had never seen, heard, or participated in such a unique family dinner tradition. It is now part of our family ritual. Fosters communication, bonding, and gives each member of the family a chance to reflect on the day... and share it. Lots of laughter and understanding come out of it.

You are supposed to list your one high and your one low for the day. I noticed as I listened to the eagerness of both the teller and the others listening that this little ritual held a lot of influence on the way all members of the family approached their day. Having the 'High/Low' game to look forward to each night WAS the framework through which each person approached his and her day at school and work. One did not mind the lows of the day because it gave you bragging rights... "My low was worse than yours and my high was better than yours." Healthy approach to the ups and downs in one's daily life.

Now it won't surprise you that our family wanted to modify the rules... by adding a third category to the High/Low... add a CONVERSATION. The family telling us the rules had never heard of THAT category. They made us stick to the rules. Only list the High/Low... don't converse about it until the speaking person is finished speaking. Only a preacher's kid would come up with a "Conversation" category.

The Bible is full of the High/Lows of the Biblical heroes. Joseph was the favorite son one moment, thrown into a pit to die the next. Imprisoned one day with false accusations, #2 man to the king the next... well, two years later. Long low. Jesus was viewed as a king riding into Jerusalem one week, dying on a cross within a few days. Resurrected three days later. The disciples were ecstatic at His return from the dead, and then He ascended into the heavens leaving them disappointed and alone again. Then He sent the Holy Comforter to be with them and us. Permanently. To sustain us through the highs and lows of our lives. Pentecost Sunday, today, is a celebration that God the Spirit is with us through all of the highs and lows of our lives.

And parenting has its highs and lows. Exhausting and exhilarating.

Last Sunday I told you of the need to laugh in your families about your own family stories and that one of my favorite drawings of Jesus is the depiction where He is laughing hilariously. I told you of my wanting Amity to buy a car battery for her 2-year old car before taking off for her trip to D.C., New York, and Boston. I told you of my mother and brother getting involved with the entire battery/motor discussion.

And the laughing was on... in Ohio, Alabama, and Holland. Last Saturday, on the telephone, Amity and Pam and I were still laughing so hard about it... and Amity still did not buy a battery.

She walked out of her Auburn apartment the next morning (which was only four days away from her planned trip to D.C.), and she joined other Auburn boys and girls who were gathered around her roommate's car... they were staring at the engine compartment with the hood up.

Dead battery.

Amity told me she knew it was a SIGN from God. Listen to your daddy. Get a battery. He is right. Get a battery.

When she told her Auburn friend Patrick (one of the ones who had been laughing at me for wanting her to buy a new MOTOR for a 2-year-old car!) that I wanted her to buy a BATTERY and NOT a motor, he said, "Oh. Well, maybe your dad is right."

MAYBE??????

The roommate's dead car battery did it. Patrick told Amity he would take her to Sears to get a new DieHard battery. Big one... like her daddy said. Oh, and Patrick told

29

her Sears could test her present battery to see if it was good or not.

For $10.

Amity, the frugal one, spent $10 to get her battery tested. Just to see. I love that girl. She is just like me. Needs to know for sure.

A mere $10 and one battery test later... Sears told her, "Your car battery tests DEAD. You need a new one."

Thank you, Sears.

"You were right Daddy. I needed a new battery." Thank you, God. God, we are still laughing. All that over a battery.

Several weeks ago Pam and I were standing in line at the Anne Frank house in Amsterdam. Long line. While standing there, I saw him and could not believe it.

He could not be an American I thought. No American would do THAT! I listened more closely. Nope, not an American. He was British... British accent. That explains it. British don't know baseball.

He had on a Boston Red Sox SHIRT and a New York Yankees HAT. I stared at him in disbelief. Soon I could not hear Pam talking to me... I was focused on the Brit who was out of uniform.

Finally I could not stand it anymore. I approached the Brit in line and told him he was out of uniform. I said, "They would not allow you to wear that in some places in the United States. " He said, "Wear what?"

Oh brother. We have a live one here. "That MIXED uniform. Boston and New York baseball fans hate each other. You can't wear a Sox shirt and a New York hat." God, it is tough keeping this world straight.

He said, "Don't care. Got these cheap."

I bet you got these cheap, I thought. I asked if I could take his photo... told him no one in America would believe this story if I did not have photographic proof. I took three shots of one disbelieving Brit while the line of people stopped and stared at us... mostly stared at him once I pointed out to all of them that you can't have BOTH teams in one uniform. The crowd stared at me taking the photo... laughing with me AT the Brit. I think that was what they were laughing at.

You can't serve two masters.[1] It is either New York or Boston. It is either listen to your father or your Auburn friends... either get a new battery or don't. You can't do both. Either listen to your father who says "Get a new Battery" or listen to your Auburn friends who say "Your daddy is a bit touched in the head. You don't need a new motor. Drive it for another ten years. We do."

One of the first questions Amity was asked when she got to D.C. and was being given a tour by David Sampson, an old friend of mine, was... "Amity, did you get your new car battery yet?"

I love such friends. Amity laughed... she can not get away from her father and his advice. And his concern. She laughed in D.C. And went back and started her car just fine with a new Sears DieHard.

Jesus told us God the Father loves us. And that we can not serve two masters, It is either Him or not Him. Very

---

[1] Matthew 6:24

31

simple. Know you are loved and know Who loves you. And follow Him.

And Jesus knew our batteries in life would get low and go dead sometimes. So He sent the Holy Spirit to sustain us. Today is Pentecost... the anniversary of God sending the Holy Spirit into your life and my life. We are not alone... we have a New Battery... every day.

Amity hates New York Yankees and loves Boston Red Sox. And she has a new DieHard. Pam did a good job of raising her. Smart girl. Happy Pentecost Sunday and Happy Mother's Day... God gives both the Holy Spirit and mothers... to make all this wonderful life possible.

Come to the altar and get your communion, look at this photo of this cheap guy with confused loyalty (actually NO loyalty), and whisper thanks to God for loving you and for giving you a mother... to balance out us fathers. I look to the Heavens and shake my head at the highs and lows of this thing called parenting. Then God shakes His head at me and says, "Now you know what I go through with ALL of you down there."

And He laughs. He loves parenting. He told us that... through Jesus. Amen.

Letter 5

Searching for the Babe's Piano

May 19, 2002

*Yesterday while the church bells were ringing and
waking up Daniel on his Saturday morning, he
bounded into our "sleeping room" and yelled
out, "This month Amity comes to visit!"*

Pentecost Sunday. Color Red for the flames of the Holy Spirit.[1] I told you all last Sunday that last Sunday was Pentecost Sunday. Much to my surprise, not one of you corrected me. Not one email response to say "Hey, Pentecost Sunday is next Sunday." I was just testing you all to see if you knew your church calendar and colors.

It is tough trying to teach you these church things. Pam provided the beautiful red flowers on the altar. The Dutch florist and I did not have a clear communication between broken English and no Dutch on my part. The first floral arrangement was a mixture of yellow and red. Missed that one. The florist took out all the yellow flowers and put more

---

[1] Acts 2:1-8

red ones in around the red roses. Red for Pentecost. Flames. Fire. Spirit.

Folks have always been intrigued and fascinated with the spirit world. We in the church spend our time, energy, and lives focusing on the Spirit world. The unseen powers that shape this world.

Amity is in Boston right now. Called us as soon as she got there. First thing she and her two Auburn traveling friends did was to board a subway early in the morning, ride to downtown Boston, be the first ones in line first to purchase tickets to the Boston Red Sox/Oakland A's game that night... then the girls returned home to shower and get ready for the first day's activities.

I am so proud of her values. She has tickets for other games this summer in Boston at Fenway Park. A beautiful huge photo taken from the air of Fenway Park hangs as a centerpiece in Amity's Auburn apartment.

This could be the year. Every year could be the year for the Red Sox. They almost won it all in 1975, but my REDS beat them in seven games... in what many baseball historians and ALL GOOD THEOLOGIANS consider the best World Series in baseball history. The dramatic 12th-inning homer of Carlton Fisk's in game six is still played over and over again on baseball highlights... as he jumps up and down at home plate, waving frantically to his ball to stay fair. It hit the left field foul pole by the Green Monster. Fair ball. Home run. Even Pete Rose, on the losing team of that 12-inning game, described the game as "the most exciting game he had ever "watched". And he PLAYED in the game! The Red Sox could have won the Series in 1986 against the Mets, but that was the year poor old Bill Buckner, bad knees and all, was left in game six of the Series at first base. The Boston manager wanted old Bill to be on the field when the Red Sox broke the Curse and finally won a World Series. The

Sox were ahead and old Bill had never won a Series... and his career was about over. Let him stay in.

The innocent little slow grounder rolled to first base... and right through first baseman Bill's legs... and the Mets kept scoring against the Red Sox after that 8th inning error. The Sox lost that game to everyone's shock and went on to lose game seven and the Series the next night.

You see... the Sox are cursed. I believe it. The "Curse of the Bambino" happened in 1918... the last year the Red Sox won a World Series. A young pitcher and home run hitter named Babe Ruth pitched and hit the Sox into the World Series... they won it all. Babe Ruth was given the endearing nickname of "The Bambino Kid."

They have not won a World Series since then. You see, they traded Babe Ruth to the hated New York Yankees that winter... for money. Traded the Bambino for cold hard cash. The Red Sox owner needed the money to save and renovate a downtown Boston theater he also owned.

Dumped Babe Ruth for a few measly dollars... and Babe went on to become the greatest baseball player of all time. Ever. The Boston fans to this day have not forgotten or forgiven the Red Sox for that move. Boston fans, and others, believe that the Red Sox are cursed for trading Babe the Bambino. The CURSE OF THE BAMBINO is what this is called.

Fans in Boston have tried everything to appease the baseball gods who have cursed them for trading the Babe. How to break the Curse is a topic of conversation every year in Boston.

This year (remember I told you that Boston was one of the teams to watch this year... back in April when the season began??????) the Red Sox are off like a jet with the best record in baseball at this point. They are 5 games ahead of the Yankees already.

Boston fans are so excited... now the talk is how to break the Curse so Boston can win it all this year. One totally consumed fan has come up with the solution.

Find the piano. You see, when Babe Ruth was notified of having been traded by the Red Sox to the hated Yankees, he was so angry and disappointed that he loaded his favorite piano onto a truck in front of his house, drove to the nearest lake, and pushed the piano into the lake... standing there and watching it sink as he stewed about the trade. He did not want to go to New York and the only thing he could think to do with his anger was to toss his favorite piano into a Boston area lake.

And the Curse was on.

One fan has finally figured out that if he can find the piano at the bottom of the lake, supposedly the lake the Babe dumped the piano into, THEN the Curse can be broken and Boston can go all the way this year and win the World Series.

Well, Boston fans are rabid. This search for the piano is huge. Two men have dedicated themselves to the singular task of locating and dredging up that piano. Thousands of folks drive to the lakeside to see the deep-sea divers trying to locate the piano. Folks take picnic lunches to the lakeside to watch all the activity. People stand and sit... around the clock. Lights flood the area at night so boats can drag the bottom of the lake while using sonar equipment to search for the piano.

When interviewed by a Boston TV station, the man leading the search said, "You know, I have always wondered what my purpose on earth was. NOW I know why I have been put here on this earth by God... to find the Babe's piano and to break this curse. This is the moment I was created for."

"This is why I was put on this earth. To find the piano. To break the curse."

Jesus came and broke the curse that Death and the Devil had over us. Jesus came and conquered all on the cross and told us to worry no more. He was resurrected and reminded us -- Death no more owns us.

And when He got ready to leave this earth and His friends and His church behind, He sent the Holy Spirit and said we would never again be alone. He is always with us. The curse is broken... forever.

Don't you love the clarity of the man's purpose in life? He knows why he has been put on this earth... to find the piano. Simple.

What would your world and your days be like if you had that kind of clarity concerning your purpose? What if you looked your wife or husband in the eyes each day and said, "I have been put on this earth to love you. That is why I am here"? What if you looked at your children each day and said, "I have been put on this earth to love and take care of you"? What if you approached your job each day with the clarity of "I have been put on this earth to do this job this day at this moment. That is why I am on this earth"?

If a guy can say that about searching for the Babe's piano, then it is probably not such a stretch to approach spouses, children, church, jobs with that kind of devotion and dedication, is it not?

Mae Smith from Boston is the one who told me about the Search for the Piano story. She and her husband, TSgt David Smith of the U.S.A.F., retired at Hanscom Air Force Base last Friday night. They asked me to write the prayer for their retirement ceremony. It was an honor to do so. I learned a lot from Mae and Dave over the years. We followed them to Gila Bend (a remote U.S. Air Force site in southern Arizona) and to Hanscom Air Force Base near Boston. They were the sort of strange folks who really believed that every assignment they had, every place they lived, every person they met... it was all a part of God's plan for their lives. They really believed that they were in the Air Force each day doing what they were put on this earth to do... that is how they approached their lives and their Air Force days.

There was a long line of organizations from the State of Massachusetts and from the Air Force involved in Dave's retirement ceremony. He and Mae gave so much... to the chapel, to Toys for Tots, to numerous volunteer and helping organizations... they GAVE away their lives helping others for 20-plus years.

Most of my assignments, I spend the first six months going around quizzing God with that most curious question "WHY did you put me here at this place God? WHAT is my purpose HERE?" Dave and Mae always seemed to have that question answered before the rest of us.

We have been here six months now. Some of us have discussed the question of "What are we doing here?" Having this great crowd here this morning, seeing all the eager smiles on the kids' faces, hearing you sing the wonderful hymns of the church... THAT answers the question for some of us as to why we are here... THIS is why we are here. THIS is why God put us on this earth... THIS worship service moment is the answer.

Under this ministerial robe, I have on a Boston Red Sox shirt... from the 2000 All-Star game weekend. Amity and I were there... sitting by the Green Monster when Mark McGuire launched 13 huge home runs OVER the whole wall and into downtown Boston. We were there. I called my brothers in Ohio on the cell phone as Big Mac put on the greatest display of home run hitting ever in the few short minutes of the Home Run Derby contest.

And Amity and I were there at Fenway the night Babe Ruth's own daughter was on the mound to throw out the first pitch at a Boston game against the Yankees... I could hardly contain myself. Amity, who has heard me laugh and cheer loudly at ballgames, never asked why I had tears in my eyes that night as I gawked in awe... at Babe Ruth's own 82-year-old daughter standing on the same mound her father the Bambino had pitched on in Fenway 80-some years earlier. I was in baseball heaven that night, sitting by my own daughter at Fenway.

This shirt is RED. Color of the Sox and Pentecost.

And I am going to hand each of you a red balloon. Blow it up, and let the air out slowly, and listen to the squeak. That is the sound of a person who has been filled with God's Spirit and is using that Spirit very guardedly and with great reservation... like most of us. We are not sure we want to trust God and let Him work with our lives. We restrict God's willingness to move freely in our lives.

Now blow it up again... and on the count of three... all of us will let go of our red balloons. They will fly everywhere. You never know what God is going to do with you and where He will end up leading you to live and work in this world once you "let go and let God." He will tell you why you are on this earth... to love fully at this place and this moment. Without reservation.

Now you know why you were put on this earth. There, that is settled. Be filled and let go and let God. Come up and have communion and have a blessed week of Pentecost. I got the birthday of the Church mixed up... thought it was last Sunday. God forgives, laughs a bit, and allows you to be gracious enough to not point out my error.

Enjoy the piano music as you come forward for communion. Enjoy this week and this year... the year of the Sox. I, and millions of Bostonians, are praying for the piano to be found and for the Curse to be broken. Amen.

After church comment... the folks came up and got balloons while being served communion and since I could not find a bag of all red balloons in Holland, there was only a bag of multi-colored balloons. Some opportunist unexpectedly specifically asked for "Yankees' blue or Chicago Cubs' blue balloons much to my surprise... had not thought about that! Also after the service, one person said to me, "Did you know George Steinbrenner (owner of the Yankees) already bought the Babe's piano? It has already been found and George has already bought it." I almost died... then she told me she was just joking... she just wanted to get me. She did. She told me she and her husband are devout Yankees' fans. I had to grab my chest... only baseball fans get the point of that joke of hers! Then her husband said, "You are wrong. The Red Sox are not five games ahead of the Yankees as you said in your sermon... they are only two games ahead of the Yankees... unless Pedro won last night." I said, "Well, when I wrote the sermon, the Sox were 5 games ahead, so that is why I made the statement. And oh, if Pedro did pitch yesterday, he did win. He always wins." Turns out that one commander here is such a Yankees' fan that when a senator from California asked him what this dream was for his farewell party when he left Travis AFB as the commanding officer, he told the senator he would give anything to meet Yankees' manger, Joe Torre. Done. When the Yankees were in town for a game against the Oakland A's near Travis AFB, the meeting between the commander and Joe Torre and other Yankees was set up. The whole hangar at Travis was set up into a Yankee Stadium replica for the farewell party... commander has had several "baseball" theme farewell parties over the years. While at Scott AFB, he was in the St. Louis ballpark when McGuire broke Babe Ruth's homerun record. The stories go on and on! God is good!

Letter 6

Chicken Broccoli and Un-molded Bread

May 25, 2002

May is still cold in the Netherlands, clouds still fill the
sky, and the church bells sounded a little different in the
mist and rain this past week. My body was ready for
spring but cold weather and the church bells told me
to be patient. Don't rush things over here, Gary.

I told you a few weeks ago about a family tradition we
were introduced to while having dinner at a parishioner's
house. The dinner tradition is called High/Low where each
family member tells his or her "high" for the day and "low"
for the day. Great fun, great way of looking at one's day
as you anticipate your answers each evening, great way for
the family to hear and value each member's life, and great
bonding method.

One member of the family often has a unique answer.
She likes to often say "I had a Normal Day. No highs, no
lows. Just a Normal Day." She fully participates. That is
just the way she sees her days. She has Normal Days.

I love that. Today in the Church calendar is a Normal Day. Color is green... normal, natural color. No white for Easter, no red for the Flames of Pentecost Sunday, no purple for the Majesty of the King... just green for a normal, routine Sunday in the church.

There are more normal Sundays in the church year than any other color or category. Most of our days in the church and in life are Normal Days. Routine days are where we spend much of our life.

Most of our time is spent doing normal, routine tasks. Dishes, paying bills, laundry, ironing, office work, shopping for food, homework, yard work, school, quiet little tasks fill the majority of our days and lives. Only periodically does an Easter, Christmas, Pentecost, or Ash Wednesday happen. Mostly green, normal, routine days are what we were created for.

Today is a routine Sunday with a routine Story from the Scriptures. A normal family story... about disappointing decisions, sibling jealousy, parental decisions, reunifications and forgiveness, and parties and celebrations.

The Prodigal Son went away from home months and months ago.[1] The father and mother wished the son were still home. But the son is off growing up in life. Spending his inheritance. Not enough food to eat. Eating with the pigs some days.

He decides to return home... he is "dying of hunger" the Scriptures say. He heads home, not expecting any special treatment, just hoping to get some of the food the servants get and to rest.

One routine day, the son heads home. The father is so thrilled to see his son returning, he runs down the lane and

---

[1] Luke 15:11-32

embraces the son... he is so happy to have the son come home. It has been too long.

Notice that the father must have been looking every day down the lane, hoping for his son to return. He did not KNOW if or when the son would return, but the father kept looking and hoping every day... that is why he was standing there the day the son remorsefully returned home.

The father yells out to his wife and staff, "Get some new clothes for my son. Fit him well! Kill the fatted calf, the one we have been saving for some special occasion! Let's feast and celebrate. Our son has come home!"

The father does not chastise the son, make fun of him, discipline him, or rebuke him. He runs to embrace his son, welcome him home, and orders a party of reunification.

And the party begins.

And the older brother working out in the field gets jealous when he hears all the music and dancing. He refuses to go into the party, complaining to the father that HE had stayed home the whole time, worked hard in the fields, and had never even been given as much as a cheap young goat as food for a party for his friends. It was all unfair.

The father told him he had been home the whole time, enjoying the company and benefits of being home. But the youngest son had been away and had now returned home. It was time to celebrate, feast, party, and dance. The family was back together again.

Daniel said to me one day as he was struggling to use our 4-year old SLOW computer, "Dad, we don't have a DVD player and so-and-so does. We don't have AFN TV (the American satellite TV system in Europe) and so-and-so does. We don't have a Pentium 4 computer and so-and-so does. We don't have a digital camera to send ePHOTOS to friends and family in the States and so-and-so does. We don't have a video camera and so-and-so does."

I said, "We are not those other families. And we are paying money to send your sister to college."

Daniel's response was to look at me and say "SO?" Ah, parenting is so much fun some days. I could tell he was wondering why HE has to sacrifice material things because of his sister's college costs. Siblings have always been that way.

All Pam and I can think of right now is that we cannot wait to go to the Amsterdam airport this Wednesday and pick up Amity. She is coming home for a few weeks. It has been the five longest months of our lives, these past months since we put her on the plane January 4th.

Pam told her we had lots of restaurants picked out to take her to. Her major is Restaurant and Hotel Management. Thought she would like to try out these wonderful European restaurants. She said, "Mom, I want YOUR cooking. I miss your meals so much. I want to eat at home a lot."

Pam cleaned out the Bitburg commissary last week. Amity's favorites will all be cooked, starting with Chicken Broccoli on Wednesday... Amity's favorite among favorites. Followed by Chocolate Pie prepared by her father.

Parents want the best for their children. Especially when there has been a separation and there is a reunification. A Coming Home party.

It may have been a while since some of you have been Home here in the Church. Come to the Table of Communion. God the Father is always THRILLED to have you come Home.

THAT is the point of this morning's Scripture story. Welcome Home.

Nolan Kitchin went to the bakery this week on a school field trip. He said we could use his treasured loaf of bread, the one he made for himself to eat, for communion this morning.

He said we could use it "if it is not molded." Come and have some un-molded bread. The Father wants you to have the best bread. Un-molded, homemade bread. He is just glad you are Home this morning.

Don't take this wrong, but we are only here in body this morning... our minds are on being at the Amsterdam airport this Wednesday morning to welcome home one hungry girl who has been missed dearly. We are counting the minutes left.

I love these Bible stories. These routine, normal moments that Jesus talked about. We will go astray this week as we do every week and fall short of being the person God wants us to be, and every Sunday God the Father runs to embrace us as we approach this His communion table. He prepares the best meal for us each week to welcome us home.

And Daniel has a new Pentium 3 CompaQ computer and a new $169 DVD player... both were on sale at the BX and we needed both... that is what God told me. Amen.

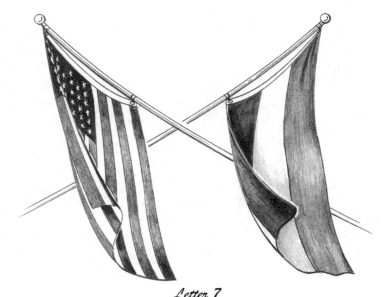

Letter 7

Daniel's Boerdonk School Letter

Who I am and How I came to this School

By Daniel S. Smith
(Written soon after becoming a student in the Boerdonk Dutch School)

Hi, my name is Daniel Smith and I'm from America. Here I'm lucky I can say I'm from one place (America) because in the States when people ask where you're from, they want to know what state you are from, but I can't say one state because I've moved around my whole life!

My father is a U.S.A.F. Chaplain, and my mother is a school teacher. My father has been in the Air Force my whole life so I've had my share of moves, having moved six times in my 12 years. I was born in Arizona, lived there 3 years, moved to Germany for 1 year, then went to Alabama for 4 years, moved up to Massachusetts for 3 years, moved down to Mississippi for 1.5 years, then I came here. Living in one place for 1 year (Germany) was unusually short. Normally I live in one place for 3 years.

Ever since I've lived in the Netherlands, I've gone to the American school in Volkel. A couple of weeks ago the American school was out of school for 2 weeks, so I decided I wanted to go to this school for only a couple of days to see what it was like. I turned out liking it so much I wanted to go here full time for the rest of the school year!

Comment by Daniel's dad – *Daniel wanted to attend the Boerdonk school so badly that Pam and I let him transfer... his third school in less than one year (Biloxi in the 5th grade plus the two schools in the 6th grade). Letting him transfer to Boerdonk turned out to be an outstanding parenting decision.*

He loved the school experience there, came home each day for lunch and at night exhausted due to the mental energy required to read, study, speak, and take tests in another language that he was learning. But he loved the challenge and excelled at it.

School was simple and yet productive academically. Each student was issued one pencil and one notepad and told not to lose those one-time issues. Daniel kept track of both the rest of the year.

Students accepted him and helped him with his Dutch. They liked him helping them with English.

Homework and studies were strenuous during the early part of the year, but intentionally tapered off as weather improved and summer approached. Near the end of the year, camping trips, canoe trips, field trips, and experiential activities filled the school days. The Dutch children greatly benefited from such sensible and intentional use of homework and end-of-school educational trips and adventures.

Daniel was selected to be the narrator of the end-of-the-year 6th grade play... all spoken in Dutch. The entire village came to see the play. Daniel studied hard and understood fully the significance of having been selected to narrate the important annual play.

He opened the play with flawless Dutch. The entire village stood and gave a life-endorsing standing ovation to an American student who braved the unknown world of Boerdonk and became one of them.

I love Boerdonk because of the way they so embraced and cheered Daniel on in life.

After being in the Boerdonk school for only a few weeks, he stated to me, "I am now free to excel." The simplicity and the wonderfully supportive atmosphere in the Boerdonk school was freeing for him.

Free to excel.

From a proud dad.

Written June 29, 2006 by Gary Layne Smith

Letter 8

Life in Boerdonk

May 29, 2002

Villagers in Boerdonk are 'notified' of special occasions in the community by the ringing of the church bells. The church bells ring to announce the birth of a child, mark the death of a person, to celebrate weddings, and on special Holy Days.

Houses, small yards with impeccable flowerbeds, windows, and cars are all kept very clean in Boerdonk. People are out every Saturday morning cleaning and sweeping their little area of responsibility. Even the dirt is swept with a broom to make it appear clean and maintained.

Movies in nearby Helmond are rated based on violence. The Dutch do not teach violence to their kids. Kids are not allowed to see violent movies. Toy guns do not exist. The village kids were having a fun water battle with each other early in the summer by throwing buckets of water on each other. Daniel ran to our house, searched and found his large water-soaker cannon, and shocked the village kids with such weaponry. Soon they told him his water gun was not allowed in the game. You would have thought he drove a tank into town by appearing with that water bazooka.

Families eat dinner at the same time each evening in most homes. About 5 p.m. When Daniel noticed that all the kids disappeared from the playground at 5 p.m. he finally asked one of them where they all go at 5 p.m. "Home to eat." He asked why they all eat dinner at the same time. One Dutch child replied, "So we can all play together."

Each village handles sports for the children. The schools offer academics and the rest is left up to the villages and towns. Simple approach.

Children ride their bikes to school year around through the rain, snow, sleet, and wind. Most children in our village are lean, tall, and healthy. Once they graduate from sixth grade (Boerdonk school only goes up through the sixth grade), they must choose a career path at another school in another larger town. By the sixth grade they choose either an "academic track" or "vocational track." One Dutch woman who cut our hair regularly had taken the "vocational track" and her sister had taken the "academic track" and was attending a university. The hairdresser called her sister "Study Girl" in a complimentary way. Both were very happy with their choices in life. Once you make the choice, it is a lifetime choice. They are not anxious about the choice. It is all part of the culture and upbringing.

After the sixth grade, they ride their bikes to schools in other towns, which may mean riding several miles each way each day. During the long winter with short days, they leave their houses in the morning while it is still dark with lights on their bikes as they head for school down the dark country roads. Bikes have priority over cars on the roads... if not priority then at least equality. Americans learn that when taking the Dutch driving tests.

When we wanted to know just how cold it was outside during the winter, we would look outside to see the kids riding their bikes to school in the rain, sleet, or snow. If they had on coats and no gloves or hat, then it was very cold. If they had on coat, hat, and gloves then it was brutally cold. So we dressed accordingly. To peer out our windows early in the cold mornings and see the Dutch bikers wearing gloves and hats was the best thermometer!

A Complete Game

June 2, 2002

It is interesting to me that when there is joy in
my heart the church bells sound joyful. The bells
are becoming family to us, in a sense.

Just before Amity came out of the customs line at the Amsterdam airport Wednesday, Daniel shook my hand, looked me in the eye, and said quietly, "Dad, we made it." "Yep, we made it through the last five months." Many days we did not know if the five months would ever pass. We made it.

All of us want to make it. We want to keep pressing on through the difficult days of our lives. Paul speaks in this morning's scripture of Pressing On Toward the Goal. He tells us to keep going until we complete the race.

There was not much I lived for as a youth in Bellbrook, Ohio other than playing baseball. My only disappointment was that the human arm was not built to pitch every day and in every ballgame. I would pitch one game and then have to play a different position for the next couple of games until all the torn pitching muscles were healed before being able to pitch again.

And the ultimate, besides winning a game with a shutout or a game-winning homerun, was to pitch and win a complete game. I hated to be taken out of the game early for a relief pitcher.

The goal was to pitch the entire game... through the good innings when I was throwing b.b.-size baseballs and through the bad innings when I was throwing basketball-sized pitches that the opposing team was killing.

Yes, we made it. It was a long five months. We made it as a family through the separation. All of you make it as military families through your own separations. One dear friend from Texas, Ann Harris, who taught with Pam nearly 20 years ago and was a member of the William C. Martin United Methodist Church where I had the privilege of serving under Reverend Mike Young, emailed after reading last Sunday's eSERMON and called it "the best of the best." That surprised and pleased me... don't know exactly why she said that. All I know is that last Sunday some parents and a brother were very eager to be reunited with someone, and it came out in a sermon.

A Canadian military officer and friend, Brian Neyedli, emailed an eCARD with pigs jumping up and down to celebrate the reunion with us this week. Parents know. This has been a grand week.

We made it.

Paul writes this morning of the Great Race. He says, "Not that I have already reached the goal and made it my own... but this one thing I do... I forget what lies behind and STRAIN FORWARD to what lies ahead... I press on toward the goal for the prize of the Heavenly call of God in Christ Jesus."[1]

---

[1] Philippians 3:12 – 4:1

So many times during a ballgame when you are getting your brains beat out as a pitcher, you think of quitting. But the goal of pitching a complete game is too strong to roll over on the mound and quit.

Often, when things were tough on the mound as I pitched in high school, my catcher Matt Timmons (5 feet 11 inches, 190 pounds, first-string All-State linebacker on our championship football team) would slowly walk to the mound. Kind, gentle guy. He would lumber out to the mound to try to encourage me. All we would talk about was fishing. No baseball. No strategy. Just fishing.

What a dear and smart friend. The fans and other players thought we were talking baseball... no, just fishing. It worked. The mind would be settled and the fastball and control would often return after a talk about fishin'. Another complete game.

Often we think of quitting in life, don't we? When things get tough? When you are getting hammered? At the job? In the United States Air Force? In your marriage? As parents? In college? Financially?

How many times have you thought about quitting and giving up on the Church? Or even done so? I have had my times. I know you have.

Our landlord and his wife celebrated their 50th anniversary last week with a four-day, round-the-clock celebration. Boerdonk was a hoppin'. His brother Henry and wife Francis came from Canada for the festivities. They left Boerdonk 47 years ago with no money and moved to Canada to start a tree nursery.

He now owns a 900-acre nursery, has 3 grown children, they each are part-owners and joint-managers of the nursery. He has contracts with the Russian government for tree orders, he has 115 employees working for him, he has given each of his 3 children a 100-acre farm, having built each of them their own 6,000 square foot house complete with swimming pool. Also, he and his wife have their own 6,000 square-foot house.

He has done good, as they say. Great couple. They speak English fluently as their second language, so the four of us enjoyed conversations in English while the Dutch spoke and partied in Dutch.

Pam asked him if he had competitors. He said he did along the way. She then asked what made him so successful in his business when all his other competitors failed and fell out of the game.

He said, "The last 20%. The payoff is in the last 20%."

The payoff is at the end. Others fall off when the game is really tough, early on. At the beginning there is enthusiasm, but then that fades away and the game gets tough. Some will drop out right at the 80% point, right before payoff time starts happening.

Isn't that wonderful? The payoff is near the end of the race. Near the finish line. At the end of the 9th inning.

I used to listen to Mike Young preach such beautiful and moving sermons at William C. Martin Church. His stories were poignant and moving. We had so much fun leading worship together. It was the best time of my life as a pastor.

Often since then I have been discouraged about the Church because very few churches compare with Mike Young's. I longed for being able to preach even a bit like Mike.

The next time I had that much fun in the church was when my first Air Force boss, Skip Courter, told me my job was to help him put together an All-Star softball team from

Carswell Air Force Base chapel. Skip is a Lutheran pastor. The agreed-upon goal was to win the downtown Church Softball League in Fort Worth. Fort Worth has at least two seminaries in it, including one of the largest seminaries in the world... 5,000 seminary students. A preacher factory. Preacher boys who love to pray and play... softball.

So, Skip, one of my jobs is to help you put together an All-Star church softball team to beat the church team that annually dominates the league, huh? Not an easy task. Sort of in the category of miracles. But it sure sounded fun to attempt.

Skip and I picked out and scouted the best softball players on base. The church league rules said team members either had to be on church staff or a part of the church. So we went hiring and convertin'... we either hired them on staff at the chapel or we recruited them on the flight line. I remember approaching one 6 foot 4 inch Lutheran senior master sergeant who could kill a softball. I asked him to play for our chapel softball team. He said, "But I am not a chapel person." I said, "Aren't you talking to a chaplain right now?????" He said, "Guess I am." I said, "Then you are now a chapel person. You will be the starting pitcher tomorrow night."

We won the league. Quite a team we put together.

It is fun to still keep in contact with some members of that historic team... first base chapel team to ever do some old fashioned kicking in the downtown Church League against the traditional winners.

We miss the United States and our friends and family so much. Yes, we do live in a beautiful country. But we miss much back home. Opening emails is such a fun time over here... to stay connected with ones we miss so much. Staying in contact with softball team members, former parishioners... it all is becoming even more and more meaningful as the years go by and stories unfold.

Such things as 26 years of marriage, 29 years in the Air Force, a daughter at Auburn and a son still eating at home nightly and blessing our lives, some wonderful friends around the world... we are nearing the last 20% in the Air Force and other areas of our lives. Life seems to be getting more meaningful and richer than ever.

So many times I have been going to put in my papers for separation or early retirement from the Air Force chaplaincy. Every week some months! I know many of you have had the same thoughts over the years.

One senior chaplain told me years ago that the fun in the chaplaincy did not start for him until the 20-year point. He knew I was thinking seriously of going on to do something else in life. He told me the fun and the payoff was toward the end of the chaplaincy... in the last 20%... again that message came through.

I told Henry that starting in the year 2004, when we return to the States after this tour, that we as a family are going to make up for all the missed Auburn and Major League baseball games by visiting a different Major League ballpark and game each summer for many years. He got the hint... he invited us to stay in his 6,000 square-foot house, complete with a swimming pool, when we come to the Toronto Blue Jays game... he lives only 30-minutes from the ballpark.

There is a God, and that God is very good. Henry lives only 30-minutes from the ballpark in Canada... and he invited us to stay with him when we attend a game there! David Sampson is going to arrange a VIP tour for us in the Cooperstown Hall of Fame... he will do so after he reads this eSERMON. He owes me. God is good.

I still long for the ability to preach like Mike Young. Now I know it did not come easily for him. In order to preach like Mike, you have to live, listen, experience disappointment and long for Hope deeply. His preaching skills come out of his life and out of his hard work at developing writing skills to reflect on life and the Holy One. Mike's integrity, honesty, and willingness to be so vulnerable to his staff, church, and congregation make him a wonderful pastor. He taught me about staying in this thing called ministry through the good and the bad. I am far from him yet.

But I have found you have to stay in the church, in marriage, in life, in parenting, in friendships for the long haul in order to have the stories a seasoned professional pastor like Mike has. Behind every story that grips the heart is a story of pain, passion, success, disappointment, and Hope.

Enjoy whatever stage you are in... in the church, in marriage, in your career, in parenting.

If you ever move to a city close to a Major League ballpark, please make sure you keep in contact with me. God has a Plan for you, your life, your house.

Paul reminds us that our citizenship is ultimately in Heaven. The payoff is in the last 20% -- complete games count for a lot in the Kingdom. Amen.

That's What It's All About

June 7, 2002

Birds are actually chirping now in
Boerdonk along with the church
bells! It is a sweet concert for
us to listen to each morning!

"For God so loved the world, he gave His only Son, that whoever believes in Him should not perish but have everlasting Life."[1]

That one-liner, that one little verse, John 3:16, says it all. That is the verse you see football fans on TV holding up in huge letters behind the goal posts during televised football games when the camera is showing an attempted field goal kick. That verse says it all.

God loves the whole world. He sent His Son to tell us and to live, die, and be resurrected for us, and God wants us to have everlasting Life. The end.

We have had a lot of fun this past week. Often during fun family weeks, some funny one-liners become great sources of laughter.

---

[1] John 3:16

We have too many people in our house, too many things to do, too much to see, too much work to be done, and too many decisions to make this week.

We have had some funny one-liners this week. Amity, Daniel, Ricky from Bentley University in Boston, his sister Lyndsay from Boston, Pam, and me. Lots of funny lines... and lots of indecisions.

Mark Blake sent an email one-liner that said, "The road is full of flat squirrels who couldn't make quick decisions."

None of us wants to become a flat squirrel on the road of life, so we have had fun pushing each other to make quicker decisions this week. I keep quoting this "the road is full of flat squirrels" line to my group... trying to get them to make quicker decisions about our schedule.

I told this group of six headstrong individuals that Michael Whittington has a great line for helping a group to make decisions. He tells groups, "I covet consensus... but if the group cannot get to consensus, I will step in and make the hard decisions." Every group has to have such a leader to survive and have fun in life.

I keep telling my group that some decisions don't require much thinking or discussions... some are simply "no-brainers." You just do it. It is a "no-brainer."

Ricky told another great one-liner this week while we were traveling in Germany. He said that the MIT football team (the term itself sounds like an oxymoron) loves to chant to its opponents as the MIT players run onto the field, "You may beat us in this game, but you will work for us someday!"

That sums it up and is probably pretty accurate.

We were getting government work done at Bitburg and Spangdahlem Air Base this week, staying at a hotel off-base because no rooms were available at either nearby base. We were also having some great fun seeing the local area... boat cruise down the Mosel River out of scenic Berncastle city, shopping for a Black Forest cuckoo clock for Ricky to surprise his mother, having spaghetti ice-cream in Bitburg, visiting Amity and Daniel's former home in Messerrich where we lived in 1993, visiting our Messerrich neighbors and touring their pig farm... held baby pigs, took pictures of Amity holding and kissing the pigs in the same barn she used to love to visit as a little girl, had homemade Schnapps in the farmer's kitchen to celebrate the reunion... it was a great three days down in Germany.

The hotel had a wonderful buffet breakfast and evening dinner. We were sitting there eating dinner the first evening we were there, laughing and enjoying a wonderful meal.

And there they were. A young American couple sitting by themselves, eating and smiling quietly. She was dressed nicely, he was dressed smartly. He had on a Boston Red Sox shirt and a Red Sox hat. Very intelligent looking young fellow. I watched them for awhile. They seemed a bit lonely to me. And I had to talk to the guy about his Boston Sox shirt and hat.

I introduced myself to them and commented on the nice Sox shirt the guy was wearing, assuming he was from Boston. He smiled and said that he and his wife were from outside Selma, Alabama. He just happened to be a Sox fan. I said, "This could be the year." That is the secret code one-liner that all Sox fans know to say to each other. He agreed... if the pitching can hold up, this could be the year.

We only had six folks sitting around our table, so I invited the Sox guy and his wife to our table. Ricky and his sister Lyndsey were a bit surprised... in Boston you do not usually invite restaurant strangers to your table for dinner.

Daniel and Amity call such people "week" or "day" friends of mine. Folks who are not in your life one moment, then they are for a brief day or week, and then they vanish forever. And here was their dad again inviting them to the table for some Sox discussion after dinner in Germany.

They were new to Germany, 20-years old, married for two years, and all alone. They were in the Air Force and this was their second assignment. They had been enroute to Ramstein Air Base, but got diverted to Spangdalem. But their furniture and car were at Ramsteim... having not gotten the diversion notice. They had no transportation, knew no one, their sponsor was very busy at work, and they did not know when they were going to see their stuff and car. They were not complaining... I was impressed with their smiles and resilience. They were newlyweds (well sort of), did not have money to call home to Selma and were just hoping things got better.

They had been eating restaurant meals all week all alone... often they were one of only a couple of families in the restaurant. And they knew no German... so there was no one to talk to. It was not a good way to start out life in Germany.

They were sticking it out in true American fashion. Transitions are tough, especially for a young couple in a foreign land. They seemed so glad to talk with us.

Found out they were going to get a government house over at Bitburg. I asked them if they knew there was an excellent Gospel Worship Service over at Bitburg. They said they had heard that, but they had no way to get there this Sunday.

I told them about a young chaplain who conducts and leads that Gospel Service. Told them Spangdahlem Air Base and Bitburg Air Base had a wonderful chaplain staff and that I am sure the chaplain staff would help hook them up to worship services and to meet some good folks.

They beamed at the thought... they were hoping to meet some folks. They gave me their names and room number in the hotel.

I called Command Post at Spangdahlem and asked to be connected with the chaplain I knew would help them. I knew he could be counted on.

He was out and would be home in 20 minutes. He was speaking at the high school baccalaureate service... good chaplains are always busy like that in the evenings. He just received his Doctorate of Ministry degree a few weeks ago in the States... wonderful chaplain. He was doing this evening's baccalaureate service.

About 20 minutes later the Command Post (they are always on duty also) connected me to the chaplain's house. He was waiting for my call... the system was working flawlessly. Good military system and good chaplain.

I told him of the family I had met. He immediately said he would call them, and then he would get them connected with the Gospel Service Sonshine Ministries outreach and welcoming team. I told him they were hoping to be able to have a way to the Gospel Service this Sunday. He said they would... he would ensure that.

Good chaplain.

I apologized to him for disturbing him and calling him at home.

You know what he said?

He said, "This is what it is all about. Getting folks connected to each other and to God. That is what it is all about. No problem."

This was a no-brainer for a chaplain with a great heart and great organizational skills. You just do it

Great chaplain. He knows what it is all about.

We were packing our car Friday morning at the hotel. The young man from Selma came outside and greeted me. He was beaming. He said, "The chaplain called us. Some people from the chapel are picking us up Sunday and taking us to church. And people from the church have started bringing us homemade meals here in the hotel."

"Bringing you homemade meals here in the hotel?"

"Yep. Great food." He was beaming. And he was going to take his young bride to church Sunday. And he was going to meet some great folks. Make some great friends in a foreign land.

The young man and his bride were now very excited about Germany and serving the Air Force far away from home.

That's what it's all about. God is good, and He does love us. And he sent a caring chaplain from the Spangdahlem Gospel Service into their lives to tell them and show them that.

Then we went and watched Ricky buy his German cuckoo clock. Time keeps going on in the Kingdom.

Isn't it fun to watch God work? That's what it's all about. Everlasting life... connecting people for eternity. Amen.

Letter 11

An Old Bike and a New Bike

June 15, 2002

*When World War II was over in Europe, church bells in every
village rang continuously for days and days to mark the
end of war and the return of peace. Peace and the
ringing of church bells go together, I am realizing.*

Husbands and wives, love each other.[1]

I married way over my head.

I know church men well enough to say as your pastor that many of you have married over your heads also.

When Pam and I were married at Edwards AFB chapel on June 21, 1975 -- 27 years ago this Friday -- Pam's father officiated the wedding ceremony along with another chaplain. Pam's father walked her down the aisle, handed her hand to me, then turned and faced the congregation and led us in vows. He had a vested interest in the ceremony.

[1] Ephesians 5:25

He is a strong person... he tied the knot extra tight. Duane DeWald's father pulled together the chapel choir... they asked what we wanted sung at our wedding. Pam and I asked for the Bill Gaither song "Because He Lives." The divorce rate in America scared me... I felt that our only Hope for a life-long marriage was Because Christ Lives... our Hope from the beginning was in Him. I had been handed the hand of a wonderful person there at the altar on that June day in the desert and I sure did not want to mishandle this hoping and trusting person who was to become my bride. Pam gave me a wedding ring with the Christian symbol - the Fish symbol - on it. Because He Lives we could face the unknown... with Hope.

Pam's grandmother gave her "Something old, something new, something borrowed, something blue."

Duane's father, the one who pulled the choir together at our wedding to sing "Because He Lives", is now in Heaven. Killed tragically soon after retiring 20 years ago when a drunk driver hit him. His son Duane and Duane's wife Dawn were in Amsterdam this past week where Duane was lecturing for Texas A&M University. Duane also pastors a church full-time... a church that is bursting at the seams and needs to build a larger church. I, and all their members, hate to see the beautiful little white-clapboard church in Kurten, Texas, replaced. But it is necessary... too many people.

One month after we were married, Pam surprised me by giving me the bicycle I had always dreamed of having. We were very young and had very little. I had always dreamed of owning and riding a 10-speed bicycle but had never had one... too much money and too impractical for my paper route delivery requirements as a kid. She surprised me with a red Peoguet 10-speed... one dream bike.

This marriage just might work.

Today we are baptizing a 9-year-old, serving First Communion to an 11-year-old, giving gifts to our graduating and deserving seniors, saying thanks and honoring fathers, bidding a difficult farewell to five of our Kalkar families who will be leaving us within the next few weeks as the Air Force and God move them to the next chapter of their lives. Then we will all take Holy Communion and give thanks and remember the Love and the Life of our Lord Jesus Christ.

What do you call a service like this?

It is called Church. A baptism, a First Communion, graduation celebration, farewell to loved families, Father's Day ceremony, communion, special songs for each of these wonderful rituals... and a pot-luck luncheon following. It is all called Church.

Church is a wonderful way of celebrating the best moments in life. We were sent here for these moments. One of you commented a few weeks ago after church that now you know why you were sent to this place... to help in this worship service. Music to God's ears.

Pam had never had a penchant for owning a bike until we arrived in Holland and she began longing to own a Dutch bike. Dutch folks are too tall... Pam is just right, but Dutch bikes are too tall. The bike shop owner in Boerdonk special ordered a Gazelle bike for me to surprise Pam with for an early 27th anniversary present. Three-speed, front and rear disc axle brakes, beautiful metallic blue paint, market basket, bell and lights built in, special 24-inch wheels... just the right height for Pam. The kind of bike that is a family heirloom... it will outlive its owners and be passed on for generations.

Something blue. Something new.

The bike shop owner asked if I wanted to buy a bike for myself.

I said, "No, but will you fix up my old one?" I came home and carried my old Peoguet 27-year old 10-speed across the street to him. It could not be ridden. His eyes got real big and as he stared at it, he said, "An OLD bike. That IS an old bike."

Now when a Dutch man calls something old, it is REALLY old. It needed tires, adjustments, lights, brake pads, and some replaced bolts. The Boerdonk bike man gazed at the bike and said, "They don't make those anymore. We have several in the barn out back... people don't want them anymore. Sure, I can fix it up for you."

Something old.

Amity and Daniel were there when Pam came home and found a new Gazelle with market basket and her name on it. It was sitting in front of our Boerdonk house last week. Ready to ride.

She got on her new dream 3-speed Gazelle bike. I got on my old dream 10-speed Peugeot bike... fixed up and ready to ride some more. Based on what the bike shop owner said, both bikes have at least another 30 to 40 years of riding left on them.

Something old, something new. You know I am not really talking about bikes this morning. That is just the fun part. This is about marriages, church, life.

We all have different dreams and different speeds. It is wonderful to be in this place called the church. Duane told me his church folks finally settled the dilemma about what to make their new church look like. They are going to build the new church building as an exact replica of the old, just larger. They are going to leave the old one standing and just build a larger new one... that looks the same. Even the painting hanging in front of the old little church will be used... a huge stained glass version of that painting will adorn the front of the new church.

That is one of the most wonderful and creative stories I have heard in a long time. Heartwarming. I asked Duane who thought of such an idea... I had never heard of building a new church as an enlarged replica of an older, cherished, smaller church. He said, "The whole church thought of it."

That is the secret. Build something big enough to keep and hold all the past memories and also big enough to allow for future growth and change. THAT is the secret for marriages. And churches to last a lifetime. Hold dear the past and embrace the future.

It is an honor to be here this morning, to have fun telling you these stories, to celebrate all these wonderful family and church moments, and to see the way God connects us all together over the years. Connecting us for Eternity.

We have a wonderful past as the Church and these baptisms and First Communion moments this morning tell us we as the Church have a bright future.

"Because He Lives"... will you sing it with me? To honor Duane's father. To honor all fathers. To honor all these folks this morning who have taken Holy Communion for the first time. To honor our newly baptized in Christ. To honor all the work of the ones moving. To honor our Savior.

To honor old and new bikes. May you all enjoy your rides together this week. Amen.

"Stupid, Stupid, Stupid, Stupid!"

June 23, 2002

*Each day I am getting used to, even addicted to, the sound
of the church bells and each day I am getting more
accustomed to the words and ways of the Dutch.*

The 27th wedding anniversary card came in the mail this week from the state of Texas. It had a drawing of a quilt unfinished and being pieced together. The words hand-written below the quilt read, "For two who piece together joy, sorrow, laughter, tears so beautifully through the years. We rejoice in your love." Treasured card and words.

I wish there were no sorrow and no tears... just joy and laughter. A seminary professor used to say every week "Death gives meaning to life." Sorrow gives meaning to joy. Tears give meaning to laughter.

He was right.

Paul writes "I am confident of this, that the One who began a good work among you will bring it to completion by the day of Jesus Christ."[1]

---

[1] Philippians 1:6

Christ will never give up on us, Paul says. He who began a Work in you will bring it to completion. The project will be completed

It was a very long winter here in Holland. Many family and friends prayed for us, sent us letters, called... helped us get through the winter. They knew we were in Holland, that Holland was beautiful according to reputation and postcards, but they also knew the winter move and weaning away from an Auburn girl on the other side of the ocean made for a long, cold, dreary dark winter that seemed to go on forever.

One wondered if the project had been forgotten about. Long winters in Boerdonk listening to the church bells toll when you miss your daughter, family, and friends so make you wonder.

But Spring and Easter came, the weather got better, the flowers burst into bloom, and we started sending some pictures back to the other side of the ocean. Sympathy and empathy for the military family serving the USA overseas away from a college daughter began to dissipate rapidly.

One person emailed us last week and said, "Got the pictures. No one should live in a place that beautiful... especially with a beautiful wife. You should be paying the taxpayers instead of the other way around. This has got to be just an extended honeymoon."

Ah, the power of photos. We got caught. The project continues. The work He began goes on.

The quietness of Boerdonk is gone. Too much going on. Military and ministry obligations in Germany, Belgium, and Holland fill the schedule. Daniel's Dutch school activities are many. The three weeks with Amity and her friends from Boston being here were full of joy and laughter and quite busy. Fun busy.

For our 27th Anniversary this past Friday, Pam and I went from planning a trip to Paris *(5-*hour train ride away on the 200-miles-per-hour Bullet train) to planning a trip to Amsterdam (1 hour train ride away) to deciding to quietly send Daniel to a friend's house while we went to Helmond for a movie in English and a dinner at a favorite Italian restaurant which sits beside a canal (ten minutes away). Quietness and being alone were the goals.

We both worked Friday for most of the day, sent Daniel on his way on his bike (he rode several miles to the friend's house... took him 15 minutes and 27 seconds... he timed it and called us when he arrived... Holland and biking are great!). We were ready to leave for a quiet evening.

Then our 76-year-old landlord named Toon interrupted. For his 50th Anniversary a few weeks ago, he did it the Dutch way. Four days of continuous celebration... parties, marching bands, Mass at the village church, breakfasts... the whole village shut down and partied for four days. Pam and I were exhausted at the end of the four days.

Real Dutch anniversary celebration.

Toon did not know it was our anniversary Friday. Pam said Toon wanted to talk to me. I went into his cafe/poolroom and we shook hands. He said in broken English, "My daughter Margaret in Handel is having a birthday party for their son tonight. They said 'tell Gary Smith and his wife to come. We want them to join us'."

The daughter's husband, Matthew, is an opera singer. He is nice, but we have never figured out why, when he met Ricky (the college student from Bedford near Boston), he kept feeling Ricky's arms and commenting how strong he was. Odd. Ricky, a football player from Boston was a bit uncomfortable (Bostonians like their space... Ricky was a bit surprised by some Dutch stranger feeling his arms).

I thanked Toon for the gracious invitation and told him it was our anniversary and that we had plans. He said, "Big celebration planned? Where? What you doin?" in broken English.

"No big plans. No big celebration. Just what Pam wants to do," I told him.

"What you have planned?" the persistent Dutchman pressed as he leaned close to my face.

"Movie. Just the two of us."

"WHAT????? I understand not what you say. WHAT you doing?"

"Movie." I played charades, turning a projector handle and drawing a square screen in the air with my hands, trying to paint a picture in the air for him. "Just the two of us. And dinner at a little restaurant."

"Film you mean?" And he went wild. Waving and flailing his hands in the air, he started yelling at me... "STUPID. STUPID. STUPID. STUPID. You can see film anytime. NOT on your anniversary. STUPID. STUPID. STUPID. STUPID!"

One, I had no idea he even knew the English word "stupid." Two, I started laughing and yelling back at him, "'Stupid'??????. You call me stupid? I have never been called stupid so many times in one continuous sentence in all my life." He pulled out two chairs, motioned for me to sit down, kept shaking his head and saying "STUPID" as he looked me in the eye. I told him I would sit down but only if he did not call me "stupid" anymore. He laughed.

Dutch people would never celebrate anything alone. Anniversaries are Holy Days and meant to be celebrated with the Church, with the village, with the community. All should be invited. All should be involved. Stupid Americans don't even know how to celebrate a 27th anniversary. Alone. Stupid.

Pam had been sitting in the car this whole time... with the motor running. She turned off the motor and walked into our conversation.

She knew. She gave me that "Why Not?" look. After 27 years we need only to look at each other. We went to the Italian restaurant first since it was only 10 minutes away.

Then we enjoyed the ride to the birthday party.

We figured it might be nice to sit in a room full of Dutch speaking folks, eat, listen, nod, and sort of sit on the fringe of the evening... while everyone else visited. And there would be music and entertainment, we were sure. We would be alone even in the crowd because no one would speak English. And that was alright.

We went into a beautiful 150-year-old house in Handel sitting immediately beside the magnificent Catholic church. Toon's son-in-law Matthew, the owner of the house, used to be a popular opera singer in Holland. He paints, he and his family live in this historic official Dutch monument house that he renovated by himself, he restores antique motorcycles... does all this with the perfection and precision with which he sang Opera.

Every project is done to Perfection.

The house is incredible. The flower garden is out of *Southern Living* magazine. The antique motorcycles are actually pieces of art, they are so perfectly restored and shining.

We went into the party and looked around for the entertainment. All Dutch parties have entertainment.

Soon we figured out the entertainment. WE were the entertainment. Pam and I were the entertainment.

The whole evening focused on us. It was question-the-Americans time for two hours. Most at the party spoke English fluently. Toon, Anne, Matthew, and his wife were waiting for us at Matthew's house. Matthew and his wife welcomed us, introduced us to their son who is huge. The son Mark is a champion Dutch body builder. Trophies and photos adorn his wall. Now we knew why the father kept feeling Ricky's arms. I asked the son Mark if he wanted to arm wrestle me, and he said, "You too small."

We ate and answered questions all evening. Where do our parents live in the States? How many brothers and sisters do we have? Where we will live when we move back to the States? How many American military families stationed at Volkel still need houses? The son and his young beautiful Dutch girlfriends moved back and forth from the living room where we were the entertainment to the other rooms where the young folks laughed and partied.

It was a wonderful evening.

None of our American friends could believe we spent our anniversary at some Dutch birthday party. We could not believe it either.

But the Dutch are teaching us that celebrations are meant to be done with the community. We Americans probably tend to be more private in our celebrations... and we miss out on so much community celebration. It probably IS stupid to want to do some things the American way... alone and without the community.

We got an email last night from a parishioner in Alabama who received an ePHOTO we sent back. It was of Amity, Pam and me. Hal commented, "Pam is more beautiful than ever. Amity is now a beautiful college co-ed... you, Gary, you are maturing."

Maturing? Guess that is what Philippians was talking about. God through Jesus Christ will bring us to maturity in His own time. He has Plans for each of us.

Please pray for my cousin's wife Sandra (called Pete). All family is gathered around her this morning in the ICU unit at Miami Valley Hospital in Dayton, Ohio. She is 48 years old and suffered a massive brain hemorrhage this past week while teaching Vacation Bible School in Xenia, Ohio. We are all shocked.

I called an old friend Dean Campbell in Dayton at 5 a.m. his time on Saturday. Dean and I were 19-year-old airmen at Edwards Air Force Base 30 years ago. We have not seen each other in probably 15 years. But he would do anything for a friend and for people. I told him about Pete and asked him if he could go visit them. He had never met my family... but he was in the ICU room with them within two hours. Retired Air Force officer/computer genius. He was always much smarter than I... he is a computer gadget man. Carried a hand held wireless computer to the ICU room... hooked up my family and me via mobile email.

My cousin Jeff emailed me yesterday on Dean's computer. "Hate to tell you this, but Pete is not doing well... Guess God has big plans for her."

That sums it up. Four years of seminary, and I can not say it better. God has big plans for us. He promises that.

As we left the party, we thanked them for inviting us. The daughter said, "We are glad you are here."

We are glad we are here. In this country. In this place. In this church. And we are glad you are here. And we are glad God is here. He, who began a good work AMONG you, will finish the Project. He promises. He will perfect you. Like the opera singer restores old broken down motorcycles. To perfection. It is our only Hope.

Isn't it nice to be here together and not alone? I am beginning to think the Dutch are right... we are made to be together as a group. To celebrate together. Let's break bread together. Amen.

Danny's wife Sandra -- called "Pete" -- died within days after suffering her massive hemorrhage. Our prayers are still with Danny and all of us who so loved Pete. One lady in Texas read of Pete's death and responded by going to church and signing up as a volunteer to teach in her church's Vacation Bible School program. She is a public school teacher and had not planned to teach VBS, wanting a break from dealing with kids. I think Pete smiled a bit from heaven seeing the lady sign up for VBS.

Note: The drawing at the beginning of this chapter is a example of the traditional bride and groom hand-carved wooden wedding shoes.

Letter 13

I WAS on that Team!

July 7, 2002

Most everyone in Boerdonk owns a bike, most will be buried in the village cemetery, most are Catholic, but everyone hears the church bells. God loves every person and the bells remind every person of that in one way or the other.

The Dutch have some good traditions that would be good for the Church to remember.

When Daniel's Dutch class went to camp for three days, they were told they could bring snacks. But if a child did bring a snack, they had to bring the same snack for all 24 students and the teachers.

If you want to invite one member of your class to your birthday party, you have to invite all members of your class. You are to be inclusive all the time. You are to be considerate and never exclusive.

The kids in Daniel's class have to take turns washing and drying (hand washing!) the dishes each day at school. Every student has to take his or her turn doing dishes. There is no dishwasher in the school. There are no lunch dishes, since every child goes home for his or her 90-minute lunch. The dishes to be done are the teachers' coffee mugs. Respect for adults, teachers, and elders is a cultural instinct in Holland.

All are to be included. None are to be left out.

John 3:16 says that Jesus came to bring the WHOLE world into the Kingdom and that WHOEVER believes in Him will have Life eternal. All are to be included; none are to be left out. These are the words that got Him crucified. He did not get crucified for being such a nice guy. He was crucified for telling the religious leaders that we are all on the same team. He got crucified for telling church leaders that this Kingdom thing is not a club for just a select few... He gave His life that we ALL might live. Church leaders often like to feel they are the select, they have the keys, and they have the coded language. Jesus came for ALL humans. A bit of a controversial approach for this Jesus guy.

A few weeks ago in a sermon I spoke of playing on a chapel softball team at Carswell Air Force base. My first USAF chaplain boss, Chaplain Skip Courter, a Lutheran pastor and a man of goals, told me my job was to help him put together a team that would beat all the other churches in the church league in Fort Worth, Texas. I listed that Sunday a bunch of the guys who played. I sent a copy of that sermon to a guy who was at Carswell Air Force Base at the time named Ron Handley. Ron was a commander with the B-52 squadron and from Ohio. Being from Ohio that meant three things. One, he was a natural athlete and two, he was an honest guy. Three, he had good taste in choosing a wife. He married Lonna, a woman far over his head in beauty and class. I had the privilege of officiating their wedding ceremony on February 15, 1986. I said to Ron during the wedding, "I wonder what every guy here is thinking... HOW did a guy like you end up with such a beautiful girl as Lonna????" They are still married, and we still keep in contact. Ron flies for American Airlines now.

When I emailed Ron a copy of the sermon, I commented to him that I remembered that he was a good softball player and all, being from Ohio, but that I could not remember WHY he did not play on the team with us the year we won the League. I told him I wished he had because it would have been fun to have included him in the sermon for old times' sake.

Generally he is too busy to email me very often. But this week he emailed me immediately from some city somewhere in the world. He wrote, "Gary, I WAS on that softball team. But chaplain politics got involved. Chaplains coached and chaplains played and chaplains were chaplain's bosses. I was a bit underplayed as there was a chaplain who wanted to play the position I played. So I was used a bit sparingly."

It ALL started coming back after reading Ron's email. I mentioned this email to Duane DeWald, who was on that same team. Duane was in Amsterdam a few weeks ago on business and we had dinner together. He said, "Oh, yeah. I remember Ron being on the team, and I remember having all the chaplains and ministers wanting to play. Don't you remember the game? We needed to win, and suddenly our coach put in the priest to play thinking it would not hurt our chances of winning, and suddenly the other team began to hit ball after ball to the priest? We nearly lost the game, and folks got so upset, and the priest felt so badly?"

It ALL started coming back. Ron was right. I had remembered how much fun I had that year and had forgotten what it was like to be asked to be on the team and then be pushed aside because of friendships and politics.

It is no fun to be left out. I don't like playing on a team if I am going to be left out. Once I am on the team and have secured my position, then I tend to forget who is "in" and who is "left out."

Ron never mentioned that to me all these years. He even flew to Boston one year with Lonna and treated Pam and me and friends to a lobster dinner. All these years we have stayed in contact, and he never mentioned having been left off the playing field by a group of ministers... ministers who had recruited and talked him into joining the team to beat the Baptists.

Religion can be awfully cruel.

Man, I still love baseball. Baseball carries me through the most difficult days.

Yesterday I had planned to work all day clearing out a storage room in our house. Our landlord Toon wanted to tile the room but could not do so until I cleared all our boxes out of it. We want the room to be tiled and heated so we can use it for our Volkel/Kalkar Thanksgiving Feast and a Christmas Open House. I knew it was an all day job to clean it out.

The phone rang at 8:00 a.m. It was SSgt Brian Van Hoose. Normally upbeat, he was most upset. He told me he had just been called and told that his beloved 22-year-old younger brother had drowned in Ohio. His brother was a senior at Ohio University in Athens, Ohio and was scheduled to graduate this year. The family was all in shock. By 2:30 p.m. yesterday afternoon the first sergeant and the military administrative support staff (orderly room staff) had emergency orders in Brian's hand and he was on the plane from Amsterdam to Ohio. His wife, vacationing in Connecticut, would join him in Ohio.

I loved how the USAF team works together quickly and expertly to help someone like Brian in need. It is wonderful to be on a team like the Air Force family when you see it care for its own.

I love the church most when I see church folks taking care of not only church members but other folks outside of the church. Makes me proud to be on the church Team called the Kingdom.

Pray for Brian. When I asked him if he was close to his brother... he replied, "Chaplain, he is my youngest brother. I am very close to him. He is my youngest brother."

Last night after the storage room got cleaned, I called my youngest brother George in Ohio. Had not called him in a long time. Always too busy. He laughed just to hear my voice on this July 4th weekend. We talked baseball. Lots of baseball. His son John is quite the ballplayer at age 10. Plays on two championship teams. Switch-hitter. Has scooped up EVERY ball that comes his way this year at second base.

I told George I had driven to Germany to attend a Fourth of July picnic for Americans there at the NATO base. A softball game was about to begin. I had not picked up a mitt or thrown a ball in years. I was drooling. Borrowed some shoes and soon was in heaven throwing. George laughed as I told him of how the old ball playing was still there. I played shortstop because I outranked everyone there... no one would argue with me when I told them I wanted to play shortstop. I was too old, too high ranking, and a chaplain... who wants to argue with God (or his representative the chaplain) about baseball? We won the game. Slaughtered the other team.

I played shortstop and got emails the next day from shocked younger players. Either they are very courteous, or they just wanted to make me feel good. They were shocked to see an old chaplain scooping up grounders, turning double plays, laughing, and being upset when the game was over.

I wanted to play forever. Pam told someone I was in heaven out there on the field. She knows. George knows. He asked me some questions about the year our high school team went to State semi-finals in baseball... one of his son's coaches was on the team that won State that year in Ohio.

Just wanted to talk to my youngest brother George about baseball again. Just like old times. Glad to have a younger brother to talk to. He is a good guy and a wonderful father. He signed his son John up to attend a Cincinnati Reds baseball camp, where Reds' players would train young kids. The camp was cancelled, and George dreaded telling his son John that the camp was cancelled.

George sat John down and looked him in the eye and told him the camp was cancelled. George said, "I know you are disappointed because I know that you wanted to tell people someday that you learned baseball from the Reds' players. I am sorry."

John looked him right back in the eye and said, "Dad, I am fine. I will have more fun telling people someday that I learned baseball from my dad. Let's go throw the ball."

That is all John wanted... to be able to play ball with his father and enjoy his father's company. That is all his father wants... to be loved and appreciated by his son John. God just wants our company and our appreciation. This thing called Life is a gift from God the Father. Just enjoy it and appreciate the relationships you have in Life and that please our Father.

Heroes and professional ballplayers do not matter ultimately to John. He just wants to spend time with his dad and wants his dad to be proud. Nothing makes a father more proud than that, does it?

Reach out to the world on behalf of your Father and let the world know God the Father cares. I should not say this to you, but I will be out of town the next three Sundays, so I will say this. There has been a young airman attending chapel the last four Sundays and I keep asking one of you families to have him over for dinner. Each week I see the airman in the hallways and I ask, "Anyone have you over for dinner yet?" None of you have had him over yet. Pam and I will have him over to our house when we return from Texas... but HOPEFULLY one of you will have him over before then. Having young airmen over to your house for dinner is one of your callings. These young airmen need you to invite them into their lives... to let them know they are loved by and not forgotten by God the Father. One of your ministries at this base is to the young airmen... they need you. Enjoy having them into your homes for dinner! Include them and their lives will be changed... I know from experience.

We will be in Texas the next three weeks on Pam's parents' farm. We will be at the Texas Rangers' baseball game at the BALLPARK in Arlington on Saturday the 27th... it is a 7:05 p.m. game against the Oakland A's. Amity is flying down from Boston to join us.

Is this a great country or what? We have a great team, great church, great God.

If we do not return from Texas, it will be because the Rangers kept me there to play second base. I have been waiting a lifetime to be called up to the "bigs"... and the Rangers could use a sparkplug player who still has the skills to turn the double play.

It is great to be on this team here in Holland. Come and have communion. You are included. Amen.

Filling up at Texaco in Mexia

July 26, 2002

*This is not Boerdonk. I heard your church bells this morning
and I actually miss the ringing of the Boerdonk church bells!*

*Pam, Daniel and I went back to Texas for 17 days of vacation primarily
so I could attend a Texas Ranger's baseball game! While in Texas, I was
invited to speak at Pam's grandmother's church, First United Methodist
Church of Mexia, Texas. (Mexia is pronounced "muh-hay'-yuh.") This is
what I said and later sent out in letter form to family and friends in the
U.S. and in Europe and other places around the world.*

There are American military families serving and
living in Europe and around the world who would give
anything to be able to worship this morning in a place like
this church. They would give anything to be able to look
at these stained glass windows, to have and to hear the
beautiful organ music, to have a Youth Minister to plan all
the wonderful youth activities your church has... they would
give anything to be back in their home church. American

military families where we live have no church sanctuary in which to worship. We meet in borrowed conference rooms and old school buildings. You are blessed with this sanctuary. I often tell civilian parishioners that the hardest thing military families give up while serving away from home is their home church. It is good to be here this morning in this beautiful sanctuary.

It is an honor to be here this morning speaking from this pulpit. When I barely made it out of basic training in San Antonio, Texas back in 1971, I looked up into the skies and vowed to never set foot in Texas again. Basic training is not good public relations or good marketing for Texas. I told God I would go anywhere in the world for him and the Air Force... 'cept Texas.

God has a wonderful sense of humor. While peacefully sitting in a little white Air Force chapel in California, a young lady kept sitting in the pews in front of me. She would always sit about two rows in front of me it seemed.

Turned out she was from Texas. Mexia, Texas to be exact. Be careful what you vow to God that you will NEVER do. Here we are 29 years later, a college degree from Southwest Texas State University, Divinity degree from Brite Divinity School in Fort Worth, two Texan kids, and many miles later... here we are in Mexia, Texas.

In this holy place. God has a wonderful sense of humor. "Tell Me you will never set foot again in Texas."

A wonderful family and a wonderful Church have invited me in over the years. This church has been the place of calling, humor, and sort of a home base. Point Enterprise has been a place of refuge and grounding.

The last two times in this church had moments of quiet humor in the midst of some serious stuff. When we buried Edna (Pam's grandmother) here a few years ago, Dan asked me to speak in the service along with him. I did not want to, but did for Dan.

I mentioned in my words one of the funny moments with Edna was that she would never serve any food on the table in Tupperware plastic or any other plastic. She was adamant about that... you served food properly on nice plates and NOT in plastic. I mentioned, in my tribute words about Edna, that Pam and I still cannot serve any food in plastic without hearing Edna's voice chastising us.

After the service for Edna in this holy place, a funny thing happened. I was told the plastic comment sent several of you scurrying in the kitchen before the service was even over... several of you were frantically dumping food from your plastic containers into nice plates... the Words of Remembrance really did have an immediate effect on you! That one plastic comment messed up serving plans for several of you here in the church. I know Edna got a chuckle out of watching you scurry about in the kitchen trying to hide the plastic containers on HER day.

Last year I was sitting in worship here with you quietly minding my own business as the sermon was nearing the end, when your pastor suddenly asked me do the benediction. I was surprised and honored and walked up front to give the words of benediction which I have spoken dozens of times over the years.

Then my mind went blank when I stood in the place where I stood when we buried Edna. Speaking in this holy place where so many things were wrestled with during days at the seminary. Seeing our own son read the scriptures in this holy place where dreams and callings were kicked around in between meals at Edna's house.

My mind went blank and I forgot the words to the benediction. I stumbled a bit. You all just stared at me, so

I did the only thing I could think to do. I called out to Dan to help me... to give me the words to the benediction.

He did what Dan does so well... he just sat there and shrugged his shoulders. (Dan later called this the shrug he learned in the military... the colonel-officer-in-charge shrug). I was on my own. He never uttered a word.

I told someone last month that you all were so entertained by watching me struggle with the benediction that you asked me back this summer to do a whole sermon... thinking THAT would really be entertaining if the benediction were that much of a struggle.

Texans have a great sense of humor.

Jacob was young, getting lots of direction from his own father, choosing a wife and a direction in life and on the move in this morning's Scripture reading. He "came to a certain place and stayed there for the night, because the sun had set."[1] He ran out of daylight.

He lay down to sleep... putting a stone under his head on which to sleep. He had dreams. Sleeping with your head on a rock probably gives you some pretty wild dreams. He saw a ladder going up to the heavens, saw and heard angels, heard God make some big promises, and tossed and turned his head on that hard rock. No soft pillow with comfortable peaceful dreams. Lots of restlessness. Lots of traveling was to be done. Lots of land to cover and claim. Lots of family to raise and teach. Jacob, you have a lot to do in life. "Know that I am with you and will keep you wherever you go and will bring you back to this land. I will not leave you until I have done what I promised you."

Jacob, I can't let you sleep too peacefully right now... that is why you have a stone under your head. You can't

---

[1] Genesis 28:10-19a

stay here and be comfortable. I will bring you back someday when I am finished with you, but for now you must go do what I need you to do.

You don't sleep too comfortably on a rock. Jacob woke up, shook his head, declared "Surely the Lord is in this place... and I did not know it! How awesome is this place! This is the house of God and this is the gate to heaven."

Edna always made Pam and me feel so proud to be studying for the ministry. She would always feed us so well when we visited on the farm and always wanted to know details of what we were doing in the church.

She never gave us a rock to sleep on. She did everything she could to make Mexia so comfortable that we would want to stay. We never wanted to or liked to leave after a weekend visit.

But she made us feel proud to be called to do the work of the Church. Edna was proud of her son Dan and his wife who both served the Church full-time.

Folks always ask Pam why in the world she ever married a minister after growing up as the daughter of a minister. She answers quickly and clearly, "I did NOT marry a minister. He tricked me and went into ministry AFTER we married." And then she smiles.

God has a wonderful sense of humor. He tricked me and brought a Texan into my life. Her father tricked me and made ministry look really easy and inviting. I tricked her and went into ministry. God tricked Jacob and took his whole life and created a nation.

Two weeks ago I sat in a jail cell. Had never been in one before. Was visiting a young airman who had gotten into some trouble in Germany. I did not want to be in the cell with him. I wanted to be home where life is full and peaceful. I was upset about having to drive ten hours round trip to see that kid.

But he had loaned me a CD just a few days before his trouble and, well, it just felt like I was sleeping on a rock. Seemed to be getting a clear message while sleeping on a rock that he needed a visit from a chaplain.

We sat there in the cell and talked about the 60's music CD he had loaned me. Talked about a lot. Then I handed him the letter... from a woman who wanted to know if I could deliver it to him. She stood in my chaplain's office and cried for him... like so many others who liked him and could not believe the trouble he had gotten into.

I handed him the letter, told him how many folks had lined up at my office to ask about him and see if he was alright.

The big kid in a straightjacket got tears in his eyes and told me he had no idea anybody cared for or about him.

Your United Methodist Church sends missionaries and ministers out every day to bring the Good News to our military men and women around the world. And to bring the Good News to guys in jail that Somebody does care for them.

I did not want to be in that cell, but for a few moments I knew what Jacob knew... that God really is with us, that He really will not leave us until He is finished with us, and there really is a lot of work to do in the Kingdom.

The young man in the jail cell just needed to hear the Good News in that cell... that Somebody cares. He needed to hear something encouraging.

Keep being the Church. Keep letting young guys who botch benedictions come back home here. Keep sending out missionaries to spread the Good News that Someone does care.

Dr. Mike Young, former teacher of mine at Texas Christian University, later a senior pastor who hired me as his associate pastor and then became a dear mentor and friend, arrived at William C. Martin United Methodist Church in 1983 or so. I love this story. His first Sunday there he told the church he was not going to be there very long and that there was a lot of work to do as a church... so he and they needed to get busy immediately with the business of being the Church to the world. Nine years later on his final Sunday someone in the church reminded him of his comment of not going to be there long... the parishioner was poking fun at him a bit and telling him he had stayed longer than planned. Mike's response was, "No, I did not stay long. Nine years is not a long time. Had I stayed 50 years, that is not a long time. Life is short... we are all here for only a little while."

I love that story. We are here for only a little while on this earth, and there is much work for us in the Church to do to make this world a bit better place to live. Great story.

Jacob piled some stones at that place, declared it a Holy Place and named it. You have done the same on this spot in Mexia... piled a few stones and called it First United Methodist Church. It is a Holy Place.

Every time Pam and I would visit Edna and Ernest, at the end of the visit, Ernest would say to me, "Let's go to the Texaco station." He would go with me there and fill up my gas tank and tell me the same story... he said he always filled up his sons' gas tanks when they came home for a visit while they were in college.

Edna would fill up our stomachs and spirits, and Earnest would fill up our gas tank. They wanted us to stay, but they knew we had a long journey.

It is so good to come here and fill up our tanks and hearts with you this morning. So good. The journey is long, but God is not finished with us yet. Nor with you. We have a lot of work to do outside these beautiful sanctuary walls this week. Like Mike says, we are all only here for a little while. Enjoy your work as a Church this week. Amen.

Letter 15

A Crappy Day

August 4, 2002

*After being in Texas for 17 days, we actually
found ourselves eager to get back to Boerdonk
and to hear the church bells again!*

It is very good to be "home" again. It was a wonderful 17 days in Texas, and it is also very good to be back with our stuff and to sleep on our own pillows in Boerdonk. Funny how places around the world for us military folks become "home" in a matter of months.

I hesitated to open with that comment because I know a couple of you families are so new here that your stuff has not arrived yet... you do not have your stuff or your pillows. And for some of you this place is not yet "home" and you feel like all of us felt when we first arrived, the fear that this may never become "home." Too foreign. Our prayers are with you during your transition time.

I blurted out to my mother on the telephone this week that we had a great time in Texas and that at the same time we were happy to be back in our own home. I felt bad after

I said that... we did not go see her due to lack of time, and I have never told her how happy I am in my own home. Felt it would not be the proper thing to do... to tell your parent you would rather be in your own home than in theirs.

Much to my surprise, my comment made her happy. She, as a good parent, let me know that she is happy when she knows her children are happy. She said she feels better knowing that we are happy in our home. I am 49 years old and mom and I had never had that conversation. God must be a lot like good parents... God must be pleased to know when we are contented and joyful in our lives and homes.

What a blessing to have two or more "homes" in this world, huh? We have "homes" in this world and we have a Huge Home waiting for us in the next world.

Someone here at Volkel commented to Pam that it must have been difficult to leave her family in Texas and return here. Pam replied, "We had a wonderful time and yet it was easy to return... there are so many nice people here to return to." One person hugged Pam and told her she was scared Pam would not return from Texas... she was so glad to see Pam. She said she knew I would return because I was paid to return, but that everyone was hoping Pam would return.

She did. And I am very glad for that.

"In my house are many rooms that My Father has prepared for you."[1] Isn't it great to know that our Heavenly Father has a big House waiting for us someday? A huge House with many rooms with many of the people we love and enjoy being with so much?

Some of us hope there is a baseball field somewhere out back of the House. Lots of time to play. Some hope

---

[1] John 14:1-7

for an eternity of classical music. Some hope for lots of singing of praise hymns. Some hope for lots of good food. Some hope to simply be loved and accepted for a long time. Some of us have so much Heaven on earth that we hope it is a continuation of what we now have and love so much.

Many of you have already heard that Amity, Daniel and I and six others were at the Texas Rangers' game in Arlington, Texas on Saturday night, July 27th. David Sampson, per my request, had done me a favor and arranged for my good seats at The Ballpark. The seats were in right field, covered pavilion seats, home run alley, protected from the unbearably hot Texas summer sun. Great seats. I had tried in vain for 48 years to get a ball at a major league game and probably would not get one today with the roof over head, but that was all right.

The game was against the Oakland A's. I was wearing my new 100% wool Boston Red Sox hat with the pre-formed bill that Amity had brought to me from Boston... best hat I have ever owned. Wore it to the Rangers' game. Someone bombarded me in the first inning with hot dog relish and mustard... green and yellow splattered all over my hat, my shirt, and the shirt of the friend sitting next to me. I was quite surprised that someone would throw stuff in the 1st. Usually by the 7th inning someone has had enough to drink, the game is tense enough, and stuff starts getting thrown. But never in the 1st inning! But I WAS wearing a Boston Red Sox hat in enemy territory, so some guy probably just wanted to bombard my hat just to make his presence known to me. I looked around to eye the guy. Usually when someone throws something at you at a game, he WANTS to be spotted... just to get credit for the attack.

No one took credit for the attack and I was surprised. Everyone around me looked like they were focused on the game, as they should be. My eyes were scanning the crowd behind me though... they could attack again.

Then I heard a coo above me. I looked up, and the pigeon sitting on the beam of the underside of the roof was peering down at the target he just hit. I swear he had a smile on his face.

Turned out it was a pigeon that crapped on my hat and shirt. I moved four rows up to avoid the pigeon crapping on me again. As I glared up at the pigeon, he or she defiantly glared back from his or her perch above me... obviously not liking my hat and obviously enjoying playing target practice with it.

After moving four rows up, I settled into my seat with my entire family asking why I left them to go sit by myself. I told them I was not going to dodge pigeon crap the entire game!

I turned back around toward the field just in time to see Oakland's Jermaine Dye hit a home run bullet shot into our section, hitting several seats away from me in the same row as my NEW seat. Guys missed the ball, the ball glanced off their outstretched hands and gloves, it ricocheted off the seats... and rolled right up to my feet!!!!!!!!!!!!

I could not believe it. Time stopped. I could not breathe. I was on the verge of "catching" my first major league ball ever after 48 years of chasing balls all over the country. Guys were running toward me. I was paralyzed.

I cleanly picked up the "grounder" and guarded it with my life. Doug Montgomery, who was with me and is a crazy baseball fan, started jumping up and down, screaming, congratulating me, giving me high fives, and hugging me. He is older than me. I was so embarrassed at his celebratory actions. I restrained myself and simply smiled. If you believe that, you are gullible! I yelled like a crazy man and took all kinds of photos of the ball, the Boston cap, and Doug and the family. It was a moment of history in our family! I am still celebrating.

I told many of this story in email and verbally. I have had more comments about this story sermon than any other I have ever written or told. Many have responded to the obvious point... had the pigeon not crapped on my hat, I would not have changed seats and ended up getting my dream-come-true baseball. Obviously we all go through what seems to be just crap -- a mess -- in our lives and we hope it all gets better someday. My Rangers' story reminds us that some good can come out of or follow some seemingly bad and crappy days and moments.

It is so much fun just telling this story and getting feedback. Several have told me they passed this on to friends who were having really crappy moments in life... car-wrecks, flunking out of graduate school, awaiting word from the doctor on possible bad news. I just had fun telling a story and God has used it to encourage some folks in some very serious situations in life.

We all hope for the good things to come. Many here in northern Europe have asked me to bring THE ball and THE Boston cap with me when I visit them in Belgium, Germany, and Holland.

U.S.A.F. First Sergeant Vicker from Belgium emailed and said, "Bring the ball when you come to Belgium. I want to touch it. Leave the hat with the pigeon crap at home. I don't want to touch it." I laughed at that one, God.

One person told me, "See. It all works together for good... had you not been in Holland, had you not married a Texan, had you not gone to Texas for July, had Amity not given you the hat, had you not gone to the game, had you not been crapped on by the pigeon... had not ALL these things happened, you would not have gotten THE ball."

You gotta love such theology from a baseball fanatic.

That sums it up. Today we have our first bulletin ever here in a worship service. Shawn Kitchin volunteered to do a bulletin each week. He said the bulletin needs to list a Verse of the Week. So we now have a Verse of the Week and this week's verse is 'All things work together for good to them that love God and who are called according to his purpose."

Pam and I attended Catholic Mass this morning in Venhorst where Father Peter, a Dutch priest, offers Mass in English for our American military families... at no expense. He is such a pleasure to be around. I love watching him conduct Mass. He is 77 years old and loves to conduct Mass. He loves people. After Mass we were in his garden area. Laughing and listening to his stories. I commented about how beautiful the garden grounds of the rectory were. He said "Yes, but what is really beautiful is to see all these people here on the grounds." He loves people to use the church and the grounds. He smiled.

We returned from Texas on Wednesday and found that our landlord had surprised us and completely tiled and finished the huge room added on to the rear of our house. It is now tiled, heated, lighted, and ready to use. It is a huge room, 50 feet by 25 feet. New tile. The landlord said we can use it for a chapel, for having a chapel Thanksgiving Feast, or whatever. Then our landlord's daughter gave Pam flowers... she said that her father wanted to give Pam flowers as a "Welcome Home" gift. We could not believe it, we were even late on our rent because of having been on vacation. Then the phone rang. It was our landlord. He was on holiday in Canada. He called to welcome us home to Boerdonk. His sister Francis told us that he missed us. I was thinking he was calling us to inquire about our late rent payment... no mention of it. Seems he really did call to welcome us back to Boerdonk.

He keeps hugging us and telling folks how we prayed for him when he thought he had lung cancer last year.

Turned out be does not have cancer... he keeps thanking God for being free to live, and we seem to be the nearest representative of God's to thank. He keeps being a gracious human being to us and others. He knows he has a Home awaiting him in Heaven, but he sure loves this home on this planet called Earth.

What a way to spend a life... being grateful to God to be alive and spending time expressing that thanks through acts of kindness and surprises.

Some of us are blessed with already experiencing Heaven on this Earth. We have a Home waiting for all of us someday, but for now it is heavenly to be with you all here in northern Europe.

It is good to be here as your chaplain family. When you come up to this altar for communion, you may touch THE ball and look at THE hat... or touch them both, if you want. Thank you for being here. I agree with Father Peter... it is beautiful to see you here. May God give us the strength to spend our time this week being grateful to be alive and to express that gratefulness through acts of kindness and generosity. Amen.

Playing Baseball in the Alps

September 15, 2002

*Each village I saw in southern Germany this
past week had a church with a bell tower
and steeple gracing it. Church bells
are a part of my prayer life now.*

Jesus told the story of when the soldier came to him and wanted Jesus to heal his servant.[1] Jesus told the soldier he would come to his home and cure the servant. The soldier told Jesus he was not worthy of Jesus coming under his roof... that if Jesus would merely speak a word that the servant would be healed.

Now the crowd listened closely to Jesus... talking to a soldier in Roman times was not the most popular thing for Jesus or anyone else to do. Soldiers were not people that you stood around and talked with. Folks were probably stunned that Jesus had the audacity to talk with the soldier.

---

[1] Matthew 8:5-1

Then Jesus further stunned the crowd of religious folks.

Jesus marveled at the soldier's faith, saying He had never seen such faith in the entire religious world. And the servant was healed.

A wonderful story about a soldier for this September 11th week.

It is very good to be back home in northern Europe. It was an honor to play softball two weeks ago with the Volkel/ Kleine-Brogul/Kalkar all-GSU team down in Garmisch, Germany. Being brought out of retirement to play softball competitively was wonderful.

We stayed in a very nice hotel resort on a lake in southern Germany. The Alps were in full view across the border in Austria. Heaven.

The hotel we stayed in is owned by the U.S. military. For U.S. military families. You can take a boat across the lake to an island and visit one of the castles.

Hitler built the hotel resort for his military leaders and troops to vacation during World War II. Across the water on an island was one of the marvelous castles King Van Ludwig built to solidify his kingdom, similar to the Neuschwanstein castle he built. It was the same castle that Walt Disney patterned his Disneyland castle after years later. Fairytale stuff.

The last thing Pam told me as she waved goodbye as I left retirement to go back onto the Field of Dreams was, "Don't get hurt." She used to say "good luck" or "go kill 'em, Tiger," but now it was just a plea. "Don't get hurt."

I was coming out of retirement because of being so upset about the impending Major League baseball strike.

Playing again would be my therapy and statement to the world which could care less about us soldiers and our opinions. We were all angry that our national pastime was going to stop while we were overseas trying to ensure the rights to liberty, freedom, and pursuit of happiness. We would pursue our happiness on our own Field of Dreams.

Last weekend it was such an honor to attend my first ever Riley reunion in southern Ohio with my mother Ruth. Her maiden name is Riley, short for O'Riley from Irish immigrants. They dropped the "O" and made it Riley when entering the States. Daniel loves knowing he has Irish blood and humor in his background. The other side of the family tree on the maternal side is Roney... the Irish O'Roney also dropped the "O" when arriving in the States.

I won the prize at the reunion for having traveled the farthest. Beat out some great aunt who has won it for years... she travels from Florida each year to the reunion, collects her "travel prize" with no competition, and heads home. She may move to Australia now to better compete with me for the prize.

I have here a photo of my Uncle Howard and second cousins Lee and Bob Thompson. All three at the reunion. All three served in World War II. Howard served in the Pacific and Lee and brother Bob served in Europe. Had a wonderful talk with Lee. He was in the leading battalion that landed on Normandy on D-Day. He told me of fighting near Aachen, not so far from here. He told me that the movie Saving Private Ryan could not capture the smells and extent of death on that day of war. He told me of being on the front line of battle on Christmas Day during the war somewhere here in Europe. Snow was deep. Death was all around. Somehow troops on the front lines were given a turkey meal to eat. He and the others had to find their own place in the snow to eat. He dug through the snow, found a stiff, frozen dead cow... leveled the snow on the carcass and that was his Christmas Day table. He was happy for the turkey.

Lee asked me to say the blessing before we ate the reunion meal... said it was good to have a professional to do it. I told him I had heard he always did the prayer and did it well. He insisted on having a chaplain. Seemed to like having a chaplain there. I could only imagine how many memories he had of chaplains on the battlefield with him in the war.

He lost so many fellow soldiers on that day at Normandy, and it took him ten years to recover from it after the war.

Lee makes the most beautiful handmade wooden oak furniture. Loves to make German-style grandfather clocks. Showed me photos at the reunion.

Pam called someone on their cell phone at the softball tournament. She only left one message, "tell Gary the strike is off. Tell him baseball goes on." I and the other soldiers and their families cheered and yelled around the campfire. Baseball goes on. The games never stopped! And we were staying in the hotel Hitler built for his troops.

Saturday morning we were tied in the third inning. We really needed and wanted to win this one. I lobbed the pitch... and the batter, three times my size, smashed it right up the middle... smashed it right into my knee. I crumbled immediately, dreading telling Pam what had happened. Then I remembered the ball. Forget Pam... crawled over to the ball, picked it up, and threw out the runner. Then almost threw up... the pain was so great.

Shawn Kitchin said from second, "Don't rub it. A real ballplayer does not rub it." No rubbing allowed.

Then he yelled it. As the fans, our team, and the other team was silent, wondering if my knee was destroyed, one of my fellow soldiers/teammates yelled out to the other team, "You hurt our chaplain. You are going to HELL! You hit our chaplain."

"CHAPLAIN?????? You are pitching a CHAPLAIN?????" the other team yelled back in disbelief. Now the other team was concerned. They obviously did not like the idea of going to Hell. I stayed in the game, continued pitching, and the other team never scored again. The umpires started liking me and our team... the strike zone got bigger now for me as a pitcher. More calls went our way... a lot more calls! We won. We scared the Hell out of them.

It was an honor to be in the States this past week during September 11th. It is an honor to serve this great nation. It is an honor to be a soldier with you.

I am glad our soldiers and not Hitler's stayed in the resort two weekends ago. Jesus said the faith of the soldier healed the servant. We soldiers and families pray for our world, our leaders, and for world peace. May God give us the faith of the soldier Jesus encountered.

The knee is fine. Soldiers are not dumb. I never told Pam about the knee. I want to play again. Shawn Kitchin told her of the knee when I was in the States. I knew God would heal it, and I knew Pam would understand. Soldiers believe things like that. Amen.

Letter 17

The Cat

September 29, 2002

*Autumn is being ushered in with the sounds
of the church bells this morning.*

"**I** was glad when they said unto me let us go into the House of the Lord."[1]

It is a joy to be a part of this place called the Church. You meet the most interesting people. You hear the most interesting comments.

One of the guys on the softball team, the team desperate enough to invite a rapidly - approaching-50 year old to play, said to his wife this week, "I think Chaplain Smith is trying to get us to come to church." She replied, "Well, that is his job."

---

[1] Psalm 126

According to her, my job is to get people to come into the House of the Lord. Not a bad job description.

Sometimes we ministers regret the folks we get to come into the House of the Lord. At Carswell Air Force Base in the mid-80's, a young newly commissioned 2nd Lieutenant Scott Anderson, his lovely wife Trudy, and their then only daughter Nicole decided to start coming into the House of the Lord on base. Scott was a Maintenance officer on base. I was the "flying chaplain" who flew weekly with the B-52 and KC-135 crews on flights. The flight line was part of my ministry. My job was to be with them... in the air and on the ground. Scott was in charge of B-52 and KC-135 maintenance on base... 12-14 hours a day, 6 days a week for the whole four years we were together there. Trudy was a wonderful cook who loved to provide homemade pastries EVERY Sunday for our little congregation, and Nicole and our daughter Amity soon became dear friends as kindergartners. Nearly 15 years ago.

Trudy loved animals and was always saving the life of some stray cat by bringing it home. I once asked Scott how he, who seemed to have no love for animals, could be so patient with all the animals Trudy brought home. He immediately replied, "Oh, she has so many wonderful traits that I just overlook the animal thing." Now that concept would keep lots of marriages together if taken literally.

Scott was also extremely competitive. A good racquetball player. Decent at least. I am not that competitive... I just don't like to lose. I always had a bit of an edge over Scott... he had trouble at first actually believing he was being beaten regularly on the racquetball court by a minister, by a chaplain. I beat him regularly enough that be soon began to forget the chaplain part... he just wanted to wax me three times a week when we played.

I am not a gambling minister, but it seemed to me that if Scott were playing for something, it might make it all even more fun. So I brought a beautiful towel into the shower room... a pink, flowery one. Nice and feminine. From that day on, whoever lost had to shower with the pink towel in the men's locker room at Carswell Air Force base. A Strategic Air Command (SAC) base where word gets around if some guy is showering with a pink towel.

THAT made it fun.

We had no animals in our house. I liked it that way. Once when I went on Temporary Duty (TDY) for three weeks, I came home and found a new kitten living in our house. I was more than a bit surprised. My question was something like, "How did THIS happen while I was gone??????"

Scott had waited until I went TDY, and solved his home problems by creating one for me. Trudy had taken in another stray cat, a pregnant cat. Pregnant cats have kittens eventually. Scott dumped one of the new kittens into Pam's and Amity's laps while I was away on business.

Scott was new to the church and I explained it clearly to him... told him be had just committed an unforgivable sin. Some sins are forgivable... this TDY surprise was not

Scott loved it. Amity named the kitten Jenny. I told Scott then that this sin was going to haunt him a long time. And I made sure he showered often with that pink towel.

When we moved to Germany in 1993 from Arizona, I called Trudy in Alabama and told her she needed to keep Jenny for us. We flew Jenny to Trudy... never talked to Scott about it. Trudy said she would handle the dirty work. Later they flew Jenny to us in Germany. Months later we got orders to move to Montgomery. We flew Jenny back to the Andersons in Montgomery.

Scott was paying for his sins these six years later.

Amity is a third year student at Auburn. The apartment in which she lives does not allow animals, but Jenny is not an animal. She is family. She lives with Amity and the three roommates. Jenny is a War Eagle. Jenny celebrated last night with thousands of others when Auburn beat Syracuse University in overtime, 37-34. (Sorry, General Kane. I notice you are not wearing your Syracuse shirt this morning.) However, the new apartment manager does not think Jenny is family... he thinks she really is a cat. So Amity got a get-rid-of-the-cat-or-find-a-new-place-to-live-immediately notice.

So we had a long-distance crisis last week. Where to send Jenny? I said we would fly her here to Holland, but Amity was concerned about a 15-year-old cat making that trip.

I told Amity to give me one day to think about it. I prayed. God surprised me and answered quickly and clearly. God said, "Send Jenny to Scott Anderson in Washington D.C. He deserves it." I was surprised... God rarely speaks that clearly and audibly to me. Usually more subtle. I said, "Lyndon Scott Anderson?" just to make sure with God. Only God, Trudy, and a few others know Scott's real name is Lyndon. "Yes, Gary... Lyndon." Now I was sure what I was supposed to do. Some sins never go away.

So I called Washington D.C. and Trudy answered the phone, which is a lot more fun. As always, she asked how Jenny is doing. She had just visited her mother in Florida this summer and held Jenny's mother... THAT cat is STILL alive and doing well. Trudy had given Jenny's mother to her own mother years ago when they moved overseas,

I hesitated at answering the question about how Jenny was doing. The hesitation in my voice made Trudy think something had happened to Jenny. Sympathy works. I told Trudy of the eviction notice and the situation we faced. Told her we were thinking of flying Jenny here to Holland. Trudy said Jenny would never make it at her age. I told her I was hoping that would be her response. She said she would be glad to take Jenny. I told her I was hoping that would be her response, "Trudy, can you take Jenny for a couple of years... until Amity graduates from Auburn?" I already had my question formed BEFORE I heard Trudy say she would take the cat.

Nicole and her five-year-old son Casey and her friend John drove this weekend from D.C. to Auburn to pick up Jenny. They are all having quite the reunion. Two girls who have been friends since kindergarten were at the Auburn/ Syracuse game last night along with 80,000 other crazy War Eagle fans.

Nicole, Casey, John and Jenny are heading back to D.C. today. Amity does not have to move. Pam and I are happy. All are happy. Trudy cannot wait to see Jenny. Everyone is happy 'cept Scott. That is all right... he is a Maintenance officer on the fast track who can take it. He has graduated as a Distinguished Graduate at every military school he has attended, his year of AFIT study, his two years-below-the-zone promotion to Lt. Colonel and he has it all under control. Except he has Jenny now... keeps him humble.

I asked Trudy if I could speak with Scott. She said he has been TDY for a few weeks. I laughed. There IS a God and that God does have a great sense of humor! By tonight, he and Jenny will again be reunited. I look forward to getting a picture of 15-year-old Jenny curled up on the lap of Lt Colonel Lyndon Scott Anderson in his home in D.C. What a reunion that will be with Jenny on his lap tonight.

I love being a part of the Church family. We take such good care of each other. Some of our sins keep haunting us, but we stay family over the years. Pray for Scott. He may be questioning by now why he ever started attending chapel. I told him years ago that God forgives and forgets sins, but I am not God... not by a long shot. And he permanently has the pink towel on a farewell plaque I gave him. Now he has both pink towel and Jenny.

Just doing my job. Trying to get folks into church and trying to help them understand the wages of sin.

Letter 18

Burning Bushes and Wheelchairs

October 6, 1981 (actually 2002)

*Today is Amity's birthday so I am pretending that
the church bells are ringing in honor of her birthday,
even though she is an ocean away from Boerdonk!*

The story of Moses and the Burning Bush is a great story.[1] Moses was minding his own business, tending sheep out in the middle of nowhere. The flock of sheep was not even his own... belonged to his father-in-law. Beyond the wilderness. On a mountain. A bush is on fire. This shepherd is curious as to why the bush is blazing but not being consumed. So he becomes very curious as to what is going on. When God saw that Moses was curious, then God called out his name. Now THAT got Moses' attention. "Here I am."

Once you get curious about things, God will speak.

God told him to take off his sandals. Come closer to the fire. "The place on which you are standing is Holy

---
[1] Exodus 3:1-12

Ground." Moses looked down... looked like plain ol' dirt to him.

Are you kidding God? Take off my sandals? Holy Ground? Moses argued with God here and later in this story. God, you got the wrong guy. I have a speech impediment and can not do anything for you. And, oh by the way, this is dirt, not Holy Ground. This is dirt. On a mountain.

We have all been "beyond the wilderness" at some point in our lives. We have all argued with God about something in life. Moses' arguing did not faze God. THAT is good news for those of us who have a history of trying to correct God.

"Moses, I am God. Now listen... there is a situation that I need you for... " Moses was riveted to that bush. He probably did not hear much of what God was trying to tell him.

Have you ever had such a moment? This is called an Epiphany... an appearance of God. A glimpse of the Holy One. No-name shepherd standing on plain dirt with plain sandals staring curiously at a blazing bush. Strange story. Ever happen to you?

I've never seen a burning bush. But I have seen some strange and surprising things over the years.

"It's a girl," the doctor said. That was 21 years ago today. This weekend she is in Biloxi. She could not check into the room yesterday at the resort because she was only 20... so her college classmate had to sign for the hotel room. Today she can check out on her own... she is 21 today and legally allowed to check out of the room and sign the papers! I thought it all was just a plain ol' hospital room with plain ol' doctors... did not look like Holy Ground to me. But, had I been smart, I would have taken off my sandals then and there.

Last week Linzy Laughhunn wrote an email from Kuwait. He looks down and sees sand... does not look or feel like Holy Ground. Just plain Middle Eastern sand... about 39 miles from Iraq. I am sure he has taken his sandals off, though no one else around him sees it as Holy Ground. Linzy will... and he will preach about it.

Last Sunday morning the Kalkar children came forward for the Children's Sermon. Time for me to teach them and help them to keep their eyes peeled out for catching a glimpse of God during the day. They surprised me. Pam asked me how I even got through the rest of church. Every child had made a card during Sunday School... for me. Pictures of crosses. Drawings of churches. Messages that said things like "Church is the most important thing." Hearts. MANY thanks for the weekly treats. What started out to look like just another children's sermon in Germany on a Sunday morning turned into an Epiphany.

I saw and heard God. Could not speak. Wanted to take off my shoes... it was starting to feel like Holy Ground... the kind of ground where one should humbly take off shoes and reverently listen and watch.

We carried that newborn baby girl across the threshold of the door into our house and she let out a scream and claimed everything. Our hopes, dreams, wishes, goals, money, the bathroom, nights, the future, the kitchen... claimed it all.

I missed much of the first two years... too busy dealing with holy things. Like seminary and church work. Holy stuff. When she needed comforting, she always ran to her mother.

I loved watching that.

Dr. Howard Stone taught my Pastoral Counseling class in seminary. Impressive guy. Ph.D. and had authored some books by the time he was 30 years old. He told us one day he looked at his nine-year-old daughter and realized he had missed it all, that she was growing up while he was studying and authoring books.

I went home and told Pam I had a five-day business trip to Indiana to interview for the U.S.A.F. chaplaincy. I told Pam I had decided that day to take Amity with me to Indiana... by myself. She needed to be introduced to her daddy. Diapers, baby food... and a shocked Pam. I called back home after four days and told Pam I was heading home... she said, "Is my vacation up already?"

It looked and felt like a trip to Indiana. Amity and I bonded on that trip and to this day that bond is still strong. You can only bond by being together for some time. No shortcuts in relationships. Time does it. Personal time. Changing diaper time. Baby food time. Dependence on each other time. I felt I should take off my shoes... it was Holy Ground, that trip with Amity having to depend on me. She came home having two parents to depend on.

Then a doctor said "Not only will you not have a second child... we cannot figure out how you ever had your first child." We were stunned. We were part of that generation that thought we were gods... we could decide when, where, what time, and how to have our children.

God is God.

I called Dottie Battle this week in Auburn. Dottie is a dear friend and member of the wonderful little Village Christian Church I served in Auburn years ago. I asked her for the name of a good florist in Auburn. She gave me the name of a guy she has known from birth who is a florist. I called Dave to order the flowers for the 21st birthday. He asked what we wanted on the card. We said, "Happy 21st birthday. We miss you." He said, "You don't want to make her homesick do you?" We changed it to read "Happy 21st birthday. We celebrate with you." He said that was much better.

I thought we were talking to a florist, but I wanted to take off my shoes when God spoke through him. Such care and love. A florist teaching me how to parent... still learning.

When she got her acceptance letter from Auburn, the only school to which she applied, I asked her if she wanted me to read to her from the journal I wrote to her when she was born. She said, "No, save that for later in life." I told her we wrote of dreaming and wanting to be able to send her to college someday... that I was concerned about whether or not a minister could make enough money to do that. We hugged. Here is the journal. The dreams go on.

Makes you want to take off your shoes. It is Holy Ground on which we stand. Daily.

Sometimes churches teach you the wrong things. I was taught that the only real baptism was to be immersed in a river... none of this sprinkling stuff. My wife believed in infant baptism... but I overruled and our daughter was not baptized as a baby.

I began to bargain with God. I told God and Pam that if we ever had a second child, BOTH of them would be baptized together.

Amity had been born in 1981 and Pam wanted her baptized as an infant but I voted against it. Then the doctor told us we would most likely never have a second child and that he did not know how we even had the first child. Like so many other people our age, we grew thinking we could control everything in life, including when to have a baby. I told Pam and God that if we ever were able to have a second child then we would immediately baptize Amity and the second child as Pam so desired.

I played racquetball with the Strategic Command Chaplain (a superior equivalent to a bishop in the church who controls your next assignment!) in early 1989... he was a ferocious racquetball player... I beat him six out of seven games on a Saturday morning during his inspection visit. It was fun to win, but I began to wonder what the price of beating your superior so soundly might be! I found out quickly. Within days, I had orders to relocate to Gila Bend, a remote site in southern Arizona. God has a great sense of humor. Looked like desert dirt to me.

On February 14, 1989 we found out Pam was pregnant with our 'miracle' baby. The next day, February 15, we received orders to move to Gila Bend, Arizona. Gila Bend has no medical facilities, with the nearest hospital being in Phoenix which was 80 miles away through barren desert.

We nearly requested a discharge from the Air Force rather than risk the pregnancy at a remote site with no medical staff. But Pam chose to trust, risk, and hope and accept the situation. Pam is one very strong woman. She never blinked. She did ask one day when it was 115 degrees outside and she was five months pregnant and miserable and we pulled up to the gate at Gila Bend for the first time, "Gary, tell me again just how we got this assignment?" But she never blinked.

Daniel was born on October 16, 1989.

Both Amity and Daniel were baptized in the Gila Bend chapel in February of 1990.

So both Amity and Daniel were 'miracle' babies. Now I know it does not matter to God... sprinkling, immersion, dirt, burning bushes... if He can work through a burning bush, he will work through sprinkled water. He will also work through deep waters for immersion. He will work through anything.

Last Sunday after church at Kalkar while driving over the bridge in Goch, I saw them. She was in a wheelchair, he struggling with the handles on the wheelchair. Both elderly. She apparently wanted to go down from the upper road to the stream below. It was a steep incline and he was backing down with the wheelchair in front of him. He was taking her to the stream. She was smiling, he was grinning. They were very old.

She looked loved. He looked loved. Very loved. Very happy. Very together.

God revealed Himself to Moses... for a reason. Not merely for the benefit of Moses. God had something He wanted Moses to do. Lead the enslaved Hebrew people out of slavery, through the wilderness, and into the Promised Land. We catch glimpses of God so that we can then make the world a little better place to live.

Today is World Communion Sunday. We are loved. Very loved. In Kuwait. In Auburn. In Biloxi. In Germany. In Holland. We are called to be together. Very together. Like she needed him to take her down to the river, we need each other.

I hope that someday my 21 year- old is loved enough to have someone take her down to the river if she can not walk herself. I hope Daniel has someone that he can take in a wheelchair down to the river when he is aged in life.

Come, have bread... in your bare feet. We may be a bit homesick, but let's celebrate. A florist in Auburn showed me that lesson. And then let's go out and do what God has called us to do... make this world a little better place to live. We have some Holy Ground to cover this week. Amen.

(At the beginning of this worship service, people walked up to the altar and took off their shoes, left their shoes sitting around the altar, went back to the pews and sat during the sermon with no 'sandals' on their feet. Wish I had taken a photo of all the shoes around the altar. And we baptized two beautiful babies in the beautiful Catholic church chapel in Venhorst... with a packed chapel.)

Letter 19

Angels

November 3, 2002

*The movie **It's A Wonderful Life** suggests there is a connection between kind acts, angels, and the ringing of bells. The older I get, the more I understand such thinking. Church bells remind me of angels and kind acts in life.*

Matthew writes eighteen verses of genealogy to ensure we know the accurate lineage of Jesus.[1] The Hebrews author tells us on this All Saints' Sunday we are "surrounded by a great cloud of witnesses."[2] So we can continue to run the race set before us because of the strength of knowing our loved ones and faith heroes in heaven are still with us. And John writes, "If we confess our sins, He is faithful and just and will forgive us our sins."[3]

---

[1] Matthew 1:1-18

[2] Hebrews 12:1

[3] 1 John 1:9

This is the first opportunity to preach to you in two weeks due to our being at the Chapel Retreat two weekends ago and our attending the Chaplain's Conference last week in Germany.

It has been a long two weeks while waiting to do as the Apostle John speaks of... to confess my sins... to finally go public and confess my sins and shortcomings as an American, a theologian, and an adult. I messed up weeks ago on a lineage and history point in a sermon.

I have sinned.

Three weeks ago I said in a sermon, and I quote:

Had to study baseball this weekend so I could give an informed answer to baseball lovers. All no-name teams. Now I know. I am now an Angel's fan... I believe in Angels.

Pam's uncle Bob Franks has waited patiently as a resident of Anaheim, California for 42 years for the Angels to make the world believe in the Angels. We have laughed at him, the Angels, and Gene Autry for 42 years. This may be their year. 42 years is a long time. They have the horsepower this year. Gene Autry, former owner and Lone Ranger, rider of Trigger the horse, may come back to life and even bring Trigger back and ride into the Angels stadium to throw the opening pitch of the World Series this year. I believe in Angels and miracles and resurrection... watch for ol' Trigger to be prancing around on the mound out there in Anaheim next week.

The emails from concerned Christians started flowing in on Monday as soon as the sermon was sent out on email. Even close friends joined in THE CORRECTION.

Judy Faurot, retired professor at North Texas State University in Texas, one who pays attention to details, a pillar of the William C. Martin Church in Texas that I used to serve, and a gentle spirit of a person, emailed a nice note and gently, lovingly, and bluntly said after a cordial greeting: By the way, as a very loyal Gene Autry fan (I used to have real verbal battles with my friends who liked Roy Rogers better), I need to tell you that Trigger was Roy's horse! Gene Autry rode Champion.

My best to all.
Judi

Another wrote, "Gary, Gary, Gary. Roy Rogers rode Trigger. Gene Autry rode Champion. Gary, Gary, Gary."

Genealogy and accuracy in lineage is very important to many American TV cowboy fans also... apparently. My error.

Marlaine, a teacher at Spangdahlem Air Force Base in Germany, wrote a friend and said, "Chaplain Smith preaches a lot about baseball. I don't like baseball that much. I will be glad when it is golf season and he starts preaching on golf. I really like golf."

We called Pam's Uncle Bob and Aunt Margaret in Anaheim, California, during the World Series. We had not called them in years. The Angels in the Series reconnected us via the phone... from Holland to California. Bob is retired from the city of Anaheim.

Bob and I swapped emails immediately before and after the last five World Series games. I watched every pitch of every one of the last five games... from 2:00 a.m. to 6:00 a.m. five nights last week. Baseball has never been better since the Big Red machine of the 70's. And baseball brought families together from California to Holland.

I called Pam's cousin Captain Jimmy Franks in San Antonio about some official Air Force personnel stuff. We talked at length about Air Force stuff, and then I got ready to get off the phone. Jimmy said he was sorry. I said, "For what?" He said he was sorry for giving me bad information a few days earlier.

He said, "I told you Gene Autry might show up on Trigger and prance around on the mound opening night of the World Series if the Angels get into it. I am sorry for the bad info."

I told him I deserved all the grief I was being given... I told the story and never gave credit to Jimmy for being the one to author the saying. I usually give credit but I just slipped and took credit for a great line... that "Gene Autry and Trigger might come back from the dead to show up if the Angels get into the World Series."

THEN Pam's father, retired Air Force colonel and chaplain, highly schooled theologian and grounded in history, got into the fray. Not an avid baseball fan by any measure, but he even brought up the subject of Trigger on the phone. He said, "Speaking of Trigger, did you.

I cut him off and told him I did not need to hear anymore of my Trigger errors. He seemed startled and then continued in spite of my attempt to cut him off. He said, "Did you know Trigger is stuffed and on display in Apple Valley near Edwards Air Force Base?"

He never gets his facts wrong, unlike me. I thought he was also going to correct my grievous error. He went on to tell me he had not even caught the error. Now THAT surprised me... as a Texan steeped in cowboy folklore and history, he should have known his TV cowboy facts better than that.

Jimmy Franks confessed his sin to me and then gave me the correct information. Gene Autry did not ride Trigger nor was he the Lone Ranger. Gene Autry rode Champion and was the Singing Cowboy. Americans rarely write me to correct my theology, but they will write immediately if you start messing up facts about Roy Rogers, Trigger, Singing Cowboy, Champion, and the Lone Ranger.

Jimmy told me the facts.

Roy Rogers rode Trigger. The Lone Ranger rode a horse named Silver. Gene Autry, the Singing Cowboy, rode Champion.

And I told them something they did not know about Roy Rogers.

Roy Rogers was born in Duck Run, Ohio. Duck Run is near Mt. Joy and Locust Grove and Sinking Springs and Otway, which is where my family is from and the area where my mother still lives. Duck Run is a poor but beautiful community in those foothills of the Appalachian Mountains in southern Ohio along the Ohio River. There is a sign there that marks the event... "Duck Run, birthplace of Roy Rogers."

It was a great World Series. It is wonderful to be back. It is an honor to be surrounded in this world by so many knowledgeable saints who know their cowboy heroes and their horses. It is wonderful to be connected through all the joys and laughter God brings into our lives.

In the book Jesus Makes Me Laugh with Him, David Redding tells the story of an All-American high school football player who later played for the great Lou Little in college. The boy had not lived up to his potential in college however. He therefore never got to play in his first three years of college ball. He always practiced hard but just did not seem to have the talent to ever succeed on the field. But he never missed practice and always was on the bench cheering his teammates. He got the bad news right before the second game of the season. His dad had died. He did not want to miss the game and was going to catch a flight home after the game for his father's funeral. His coach, knowing he was not going to play the kid anyway, encouraged him to miss the game and go on home. The kid did so.

The next week the kid pleaded to start in the game. Coach Little, a compassionate person, knowing his team were the underdogs anyway, as a gesture, put him on defense. Kid plowed through and tackled the runner, saving a touchdown. Coach let him stay in on defense. After several tackles, he begged to play offense. Coach complied as a gesture again. Kid ran a punt return for a touchdown, seeming to be playing with a mission. He scored two touchdowns plus making several key tackles on defense. He was named Player of the Game. Such play earned him a starting position the next game.

He ended up having such a year he won All-American honors for his incredible play and turn around. Coach asked him at the end of the year what happened when he went home for his dad's funeral... what had inspired him so and seemed to have given him such incredible motivation and talent.

Kid said, "Oh, nothing happened at the funeral. But you see, my dad has been blind for years and never got to see me play football in high school. When you played me in that game after the funeral that was the first game my dad has ever got to see me play. He now can see from above. He now gets to watch me play. I have fun playing knowing he can see now."

The next world is watching. We are playing for keeps.

Ah, another one of those Angel stories.

I must confess. I believe in these kinds of stories. Nothing else in this life makes more sense.

Come forward on this All Saints' Day and have some communion. We are blessed to be surrounded by so many good memories and stories and to be watched over by those gone before us to the next world. God is good.

But I still don't think the Saints or the Cowboys will make it to the Super Bowl. I think it is the year of the Dolphins.

Letter 20

Passed Over in Life

November 10, 2002

There are sad moments and days in life. The Boerdonk church bells sounded a bit sad this morning.

This morning's Lectionary Reading is an interestingly different sort of story. Jesus tells of ten young ladies, ten virgins, each who hoped to be selected by the groom to become a new wife.[1] The ten were going to wait all night with their lamps being lit to show the groom where to look. Half of them brought enough oil for the night, five did not. The groom, typical man that he was, was late to the Selection Party. "The bridegroom was long delayed" is the wording of the Scripture. Long delayed. Nice wording. Anyway, all the potential brides fell asleep... not a bad plan. If the guy is not on time, just go to sleep. Not a bad backup plan. The five with little oil ran out of oil because the groom was late.

So in the middle of the night, after being "long delayed," the groom shows up. The five who were short of oil tried to borrow some from the others. You would have thought Jesus was going to say the five with oil should share with the five who ran out of oil. But he does not. He surprises the listener and says that every woman should go find her own oil. Each person is responsible for preparing for herself. Every woman for herself in this husband-searching game.

---

[1] Matthew 25:1-13

133

The wedding party search continued with just the five who had planned ahead and brought enough oil.

Jesus is saying through this story to plan ahead, stay awake, and be prepared. You know not what hour or day you will be called. And you are responsible for your own life.

One friend and I try to pass on to our children what we call the "open approach to life and career." Keep lots of doors open, burn as few bridges as possible, have lots of options in life. Don't limit God by limiting your options. Have lots of doors to choose from. Plan as if you may need any one of the options at any time. Bring lots of oil for your lamps.

There may be long nights ahead and bring your own oil, Jesus would say.

This past month has been so interesting as a pastor. Emails keep coming in about the error I made concerning Roy Rogers and the horse Trigger and the Angels and the World Series. A Canadian friend, Brian Neyedli, wrote me and said even he caught the error via email, but he did not feel he as a Canadian should be correcting an American concerning the American's own folk heroes. Brian used to listen to Roy Rogers on the radio in Canada.

Phil Garrant from Hill Air Force Base wrote and said he was glad I had folks in my world to whom I was accountable... he just let the Roy Rogers and Trigger comment go and figured he would let the editor catch it someday when the sermon was printed in book form. Funny answer. Loved the diplomacy.

It really is an honor to serve as chaplain to such thoughtful folks. Folks who can write with wit and share with such sensitivity.

Linzy Laughhunn, chaplain deployed to Kuwait and one who would never have made the Trigger error I made in a sermon, wrote and said, "Well, at least you know the folks are reading your stuff if they caught the Trigger error." Linzy always has a refreshing way of looking at things.

As a pastor and chaplain, you never know what kind of party you may be invited to. You never know when they will be held, you never know the hour or day.

Last night Pam and I went to our first ever "Chiefs Passed Over Party" at Volkel. Mark Blake and Bill Hartley both were waiting for the list to come out this past week to tell them whether or not they had each been promoted to Chief Master Sergeant, the highest enlisted rank in the Air Force. They both like parties and wanted to plan ahead... 'cept they did not know the outcome of the list ahead of time. Being good party folks, they came up with a plan.

They planned a "Chiefs or Chiefless" Party last night, covering both bets. Catered it, sent out invitations. We all laughed at the novelty of it. The list came out and neither of them made Chief. Both were near the top of the list, but neither close enough.

So we attended the "Chiefless Passover Party" last night. I loved the idea of it. It was the first Passover Party in my 23 years of active duty I had ever heard of or attended. The rank of Chief was on the cake and on the posters... all with a line drawn through the rank to indicate 'NOT'.

Now THAT was having a backup plan in life! We had fun, good food, and laughter. Mark and Bill are old enough in life they get it... life is too short to fret the small stuff like a passover. Mark said in his "passover speech" that the good news is he gets to stay at Volkel another year and work with great people. Bill said now they don't have to worry about moving and can put up curtains and pictures on the walls in his house... they had just moved here and would have had to move again had he made Chief.

Bring enough oil for the night.

I told them that during my seven years of enlisted time in the Air Force I would have gone broke paying for passover parties if I had a party every time I got "passed over" (failed to make promotion) to Staff Sergeant. The only way I could ever get promoted in the military was to be commissioned as a chaplain officer! Getting promoted in the enlisted ranks is difficult! They loved that one!

Tonight is another first for our family. The Protestant and Catholic Volkel and Kalkar folks are having a Clergy Appreciation Night for Father Peter, Reverend DeVries (the missionary who is also a contract clergy for us), and our family. All three congregations are meeting for one Clergy Appreciation Service. They planned it, not us. You know no priest or preacher would plan a huge gathering and have NO sermon and NO offering... the perfect service according to lay folks... no sermon and no offering... just some folks giving short speeches of tribute to our families and us. We have never been a part of anything like this. No preaching for the three of us. Clever and diplomatic way for the parishioners to get a week off from listening to a sermon. Meeting at the beautiful Venhorst St John's Catholic Church at 5:00 p.m. with a reception following,

Generals Colin Powell and Norman Schwarzkopf said in their respective books they always had one foot in the military and one foot out of the military... and they both felt such a plan made them better officers. They had internal tensions and questions concerning what they were doing in life... and options were always being considered. And they felt that made them more awake and engaged and productive.

Being one who has always had one foot in the ministry and one out as well as one who has one foot in the military and one out, Powell's and Schwarzkopf's approach make sense to me.

I have a counseling session in Belgium Tuesday at Kleine-Brogul. Young man is wrestling with God... feels God is calling him into the circle of the ministry and the chaplaincy. Pray for him. As one police officer in Mississippi told me years ago when he was writing out a speeding ticket to me, and I was trying to convince him otherwise, telling him I was in seminary and without money... he said, "Oh, you gonna be a preacher???? Then this ticket will be no problem compared to the problems you are going to have in life." And he wrote out the whole ticket and counted every mile over the speed limit I was going... and he did it all with a devilish grin! Pray for this young man in Belgium.

We need him.

Weeks like this past week and moments like tonight make me glad to have stayed within the circles God has called us.

Come and have communion. And take lots of oil with you this week. And be ready to have a party when life passes you over. As Chaplain Tom Heather told a group of passed-over parishioners at Gila Bend chapel years ago, "When you stand before God someday, God is not going to ask you what rank you made. He is going to ask you what good you did in life. Did you benefit the community? Did you make your world a little better place to live? Did you do your part? Did you do your duty? Those will be the questions. Go, live fully and remember what questions you will be asked and which ones you won't be asked."

We all will be passed over eventually in career and in life. Have enough oil for that moment. And then there will be God waiting for us. I am honored to be in uniform with you and to serve communion to you on this Veteran's Day weekend. Amen.

Letter 21

"Hey Prof, Pray for Me"

November 24, 2002

*Bells ring in school to mark the beginning and end of class.
I heard a story once of a young new chaplain who was
attending the Air Force chaplain school. These Chaplain
students were permitted to use the restroom after
the bell rang, signaling class break. The chaplain
commented at graduation that he did not know
if he would ever be able to use the bathroom
again without a preceeding bell signal!
Schools and bells go together often.*

Thankfulness.

Let's be thankful for the 17 teenagers who showed up
from two countries last night for our first-ever Chapel All-
Night Youth Lock-In on base. When Pam and I left early last
night, music was blaring, food was piled high on the tables,
kids were making new friends, there was much laughter,
and even the seven adult volunteers were laughing in spite
of facing a night of no sleep. We parents should thank
God for such an opportunity the adult volunteers gave our
youth last night to fellowship and make good memories

139

within the church circle. They were to go home to sleep at 10:00 a.m. this morning.

Before we get to the scripture stuff... let me make sure you know the good news. Auburn University, the underdogs with many injuries and their #1, #2, and #3 running backs out with injuries so they had to use their # 4 running back in the game... beat 9th ranked Alabama last night 17-7. Our only daughter and lots of our money go to Auburn... we are invested heavily in that Auburn football team. Last Sunday in the sermon I said that Pam and I have not lost a dime in the stock market because we did not have a dime invested in it anymore. One parishioner came to my office this week, pointed to the photo on my desk of Amity and Daniel and me at Fenway Park and said, "THAT is what you are investing in. Those two kids, huh?" What a wonderful thing to say.

Amity called at 5:00 a.m. this morning... the celebration was still going strong at Toomer's Corner at Auburn, the intersection where the post-game celebrations happen and where rolls of toilet paper fill the trees on victory night. Amity said it was raining toilet paper... toilet paper covers trees, fire hydrants, streets... everything. And the game was not even AT Auburn... it was an away game! We could hardly hear her... but the call was wonderful. There's so much for which to be thankful in life.

Back to scriptures and Thanksgiving.

These were ten rejects in life-all had leprosy.[1] In those days they were condemned to spend their miserable days isolated from the rest of humanity by being confined to a lepers' colony so that the highly contagious and deadly disease would not be passed on to others. They were rotting to death as the horrible disease literally, slowly, ate

---

[1] Luke 17:11-19

their skin and lives. They were prevented by law from even approaching other human beings.

Jesus was passing through their neighborhood, which He seemed to have a tendency to do. They risked approaching him. They cried out, "Jesus. Master, have mercy on us." A pitiful plea. He saw them, told them to go to the synagogue and show themselves to the priest.

Great. Jesus sent the problems to the church. What in the world is Jesus thinking? Jesus creates problems for the church and the church leadership by sending such problems our way. I wish, as a pastor, that Jesus would just take care of such problems and leave the church out of it. We have enough stuff on our plates without Jesus sending more problems our way. Any chaplain, youth director, Christmas Play director, Sunday School teacher, church budget director, any church staff member will tell you... we have our hands full without Jesus sending the church MORE problems.

In my first church out of seminary, I worked for Reverend Mike Young. Wonderful human being. Loved the church and loved what he was doing in life. Healthy, functional, came from a good Baptist home in Texas. He loved being a minister. He made it look so easy. I loved going to work because of him and folks loved attending worship every Sunday because of him. Different, huh?

One day I, as a newly-ordained minister, commented to him that I was getting tired of dealing with all the weird problems and difficult people our rapidly growing church seemed to attract. He said something like, "Better get used to it. The church is here for sick people. Jesus came to heal the sick... that is who He brings into the church. That is why we are here... to help the sick. Get used to it." And he grinned. No discussion.

I think it was Will Rogers who said he would never join any private club that would have him as a member. Jesus brings some weird ones into the church. And we are they.

Surprising thing happened on the way to the synagogue. All ten of them were healed. One realized it. Apparently the other nine did not even realize they were healed. Luke the physician, who was a doctor himself, tells this story. You know Luke must have marveled at hearing this story of healing. Luke indicates they were healed and did not even realize it!

The one who realized he was healed turned and went back to Jesus. He was a Samaritan to boot... from the wrong side of the tracks. But he went back and thanked Jesus. The other nine went on their way.

I would have been one of the nine who got healed, ran away and never looked back. Never thinking of taking the time to thank the Healer. I got stuff to do. Had I been healed, I would have never looked at Jesus in my rear-view mirror. Too much time to make up. Get back home to my wife and kids. Go see the Reds or the Boston Red Sox play in a World Series. Check my email at home. Read. Play with the dog. Ride my bike. Too many things to do to take time to go back and say thanks. Get back to the office. Check on the college scores.

Duane DeWald told a story recently at our chapel retreat.

He told a great story out of the classroom. He teaches Marketing classes at Texas A&M University and the classes are quite demanding for the students. He says panicked students, who know he is also a pastor of a church, often come up to him before a big test and say, "Hey Prof, will you please pray for me concerning this test? I am really nervous about it and need you to pray for me."

Duane says he writes down the names of the students who ask him to pray for them... because be says he takes every prayer request seriously and that when someone asks him to pray for them he always makes sure he does just that. Writes down their name and prays for them.

He says often the students who were so scared of the tests that they actually asked the professor to pray for them will be ecstatic when they get their grades back and see they passed the test. He says they run up to him and show him their grades and say things like "Man, I nailed that test, didn't I?" Or "Aren't you proud of me?" Or "Look what I did. I stayed up all night and crammed, and all my work paid off."

Duane says that in the 14 years of teaching and actually praying for students who request such a thing, one thing is very interesting. He says not one student has ever come up after requesting prayer, and said, "Thanks for praying for me. I don't think I could have done it without your prayers. Thanks, Prof." They look and see their leprosy gone and look and see their passing grade and bounce on their merry way, proud of what they have done for themselves. Look at what I did... how I succeeded... how I studied. And we are they.

I am glad Jesus came through MY neighborhood and sent me to the "priest." To the church. The leper realized he had been healed. We cannot do this test called Life alone.

We can give thanks for what we don't have sometimes also. Once, years ago when our daughter was about 12 and our son about 5, we were talking a lot about giving thanks for things in life at both home and church. On a Saturday morning, I took our daughter's TV out of her room as a discipline action... on a Saturday morning taking away her cartoons was about the worst thing I could do as a father. Daniel watched the whole thing... the tension, the removal of the TV, the crying. He looked at me and said, "I am glad I don't have a TV in my room." Being thankful means different things to different people.

Let's go around the congregation and stand and tell one thing you are thankful for this morning. Then this week write one person a letter and tell him or her how thankful you are for what they mean to you.

Aren't you glad Jesus came through your neighborhood to heal you and give you life? And aren't you glad you are not an Alabama fan? Amen.

Letter 22

Family Christmas Letter

November 30, 2002

*The sounds of Christmas should always
include church bells & sleigh bells.*

Merry Christmas from Boerdonk! From our little village with one church (with bells), one bike shop, one cemetery, one school, and one grocery truck that delivers groceries on Wednesdays and Saturdays. 180 houses. Simple life. We take a horse and buggy to eat at a restaurant along the nearby canal when American guests visit. WWII was fought in Boerdonk. Dutch prefer American presence and protection over other possibilities history has "offered" their idyllic country.

Farmers here really do wear wooden shoes (wood is the best material to keep their feet dry from the wet farmland plus wooden shoes also protect the farmer's feet from being stepped on by dairy cows when working in the barn). There really are 937 working windmills in Holland. Tulip heaven! Pam now owns a real Dutch bike, so she is "in."

Daniel survived three schools last year. He started sixth grade in Biloxi, then the U.S.A.F. transferred us here to the Netherlands (Holland) in November to start up a new chaplain position in northern Europe. He attended the American run DoDD school for a few months and then asked us if he could apply to attend the Dutch school in Boerdonk. He was already quite fluent in Dutch after only four months and the Dutch school faculty were so impressed with his fluency and his attitude they allowed him to transfer to the Boerdonk school called Sint Nikolaas (Dutch spelling). Daniel loved it and the school used him to help Dutch children practice English and they helped him learn more Dutch. He loved that experience and we are so proud of his courage... all homework and schoolwork was in Dutch. He had to ask Dutch neighbors to assist him sometimes on his homework because Pam and I were of NO use to him! He was so fluent in Dutch that the faculty selected him to narrate the end-of-the-year school play, which was attended by the whole village. After he spoke flawless Dutch the first paragraph of the narration, the villagers gave a standing ovation! Daniel beamed.

Sint Nikolaas School only goes through the 6th grade, so this year he attends the Dutch International Secondary School Eindhoven (ISSE) which is a one-hour bus ride for him. Three hundred students from 43 different nations attend the school with university-style curriculum. He and ten other American military students take 13 classes including three languages – Spanish, Dutch, and English. He is thriving. He has a most wonderful teacher named Erika Elkady who is Dutch and studied as an exchange graduate student for one year in American History at the University of Pennsylvania. She is remarkable with the students, an absolutely gifted teacher who brings compassion, passion for teaching, intellect, inquisitiveness, and zeal to each classroom she leads. Daniel got upset when he realized he is taking more classes at ISSE than Amity is taking at Auburn each semester!

Our large farmhouse, built in 1916, is large enough to hold Daniel's new drum set. Pam enjoys listening to him practice... the love of a mom is beyond measure. With Boerdonk being so quiet, we livened it up a bit with the drums and with bringing our nuclear-powered dog Baloo over in September.

Amity visits us twice a year from Auburn, is an escort to "Aubie the Tiger" (Auburn mascot) at the football and baseball games (I am so proud of her love of THE GAME), and is in her third year at Auburn.

Pam works for the U.S. government now as the School Liaison Officer to represent the educational concerns of military families with students at the International Schools, Department of Defense Dependent Schools, and the local schools in northern Europe. Following 9/11, her main issues are the students' safety and protection concerns on the long and vulnerable bus rides and in unprotected schools in civilian communities. She has her hands full, but the children and parents could not have a stronger advocate. She has their total confidence during these unsettling times. The world here is finding what it is like to deal with a smiling Texan school teacher of strong constitution who is relentless when it comes to her concern for the needs of the children in school.

We travel weekly to meet the religious and educational needs of U.S.A.F. and NATO military personnel and families in northern Germany, Belgium, and Holland so we get to see some incredibly beautiful parts of the world. Lace and chocolates in Belgium and the Alps in southern Germany where we will take Amity skiing over the Christmas holidays come to mind at this moment!

Letters from Boerdonk

We will be celebrating the birth of our Lord by having a joint Dutch/English Catholic/Protestant Christmas Eve Service in the majestic St. John's Catholic Church in the village of Venhorst. Father Peter, a Dutch priest, and I will serve Communion to Dutch and Americans (he to the Catholics and I to the Protestants) as we sing carols accompanied by a live orchestra. Amity will be here and it will be a wonderful Christmas... and we got cards out this year! Merry Christmas!

Letter 23

Sinta Klaus

December 8, 2002

Sinta Klaus arrives in Boerdonk accompanied by the ringing of the church bells. His helpers, called Swartz Pete, hide on the roof of the church fellowship hall, waiting to surprise the village children and throw them treats from the roof of the church.

"In the beginning was the Word, and the Word was with God, and the Word was God. He was in the beginning with God. All things were made through Him, and without Him was not anything made that was made. In Him was life and the life was the light of men and the light shines in the darkness and the darkness has not overcome it.

There was a man sent from God whose name was John. He came for testimony, to bear witness to the Light, that all might believe through him. He was not the light, but came to bear witness to the light."[1]

God makes all good things in life happen. Celebrations, Birth of Christ and Aging. It is all good, and the author is God. So says John the gospel writer.

Old Christmas Stories from an Old Man.

The core of this morning's Blessing of the Candy Canes Service came from Pam's father who conducted this Blessing Service on December 5, 1987, in a church in Frankfurt, Germany. He was a missionary for the United Methodist Church then, having just retired from 30 years of missionary work to U.S. military folks while a chaplain on active duty. He retired reluctantly after his 30 years and then went to work as a missionary for the U.S. United Methodist Church in Germany. He worked in the office of the German bishop in Frankfurt and ministered to all the English-speaking Methodists in Europe.

He was building the Kingdom and did so through this Blessing Service. He would have been here this morning, visiting us in Europe and perhaps preaching this sermon, but he is now building a house in Texas. Has been for two years. Just had surgery this past week... building a house for two years has its price. We called this week to see how he was doing.

He did not want to talk about himself. His focus was, "Gary, I can't believe how old you are." And I paid good money to make this call and to hear such words.

One family gave me Dutch cheese marked OLD cheese with the word OLD in large letters and underlined.

Have not been able to get away from this age thing all week. Prior to this week, folks called me "honorable

[1] John 1:1-15

150

Chaplain Smith" or "distinguished Chaplain Smith" or "Mr." or some title with dignity and respect. Now even kids are calling me simply 'old man.' One first grade kid, who obviously comes from a home where respect for elders is NOT taught, even called me "crazy old fat man" on my birthday. After turning 50 Thursday, without consciously meaning to, I even began answering the phone "Old Man" instead of "Chaplain Smith." Pam's dad called Saturday, I answered the phone "old man" and he said, "Given up, huh?" He knew.

It has been too much fun. Turning 50 sure beats the alternative.

Received an email this week. 24-font print. It was entitled "50,000000000000" and reads:

Gary,

Where you put the decimal point makes a big difference!

Hope you can read this larger font. Do I need to type louder? I said, do . . . I . . . .
need. . . .to. . . . . .type . . .
.LOUDER??????

Take Care not to fall and break a hip.
Bones heal slowly at your age.
Duane

That from a lifelong friend.

My mom taught me to love the Old Story of Christmas and to love the jolly old man named Saint Nicholas (Dutch spelling is Nicolaas). Always have. She made him so real and fun in our home growing up. I love collecting figurines, statues, and carvings of Saint Nicholas. Here is one given me this week... a Santa with a bobbing head and body. It is from Texas... you put such bobbing figures in the rear window of your vehicle (truck) in Texas. Here is one entitled Santa Kneeling at the Manger that Pranitan gave us in Massachusetts. Pranitan is like a second daughter to us... she is a dear friend of Amity's and lived with us their senior year in Massachusetts after her family got transferred. Like that symbol. Here is another beautiful Santa bearing gifts on his back, holding a Christmas wreath in one hand, and holding a church in the other. It is entitled "The Peacemaker." Isn't that a wonderful message to the world? That one came from Norman and Wendy Johnson, Air Force colonel and Air Force wife... who never give up praying for peace on earth and who give their lives and energies working toward that hope as an Air Force family.

It takes a lot of work, vision, and tenacity to keep passing on the Story some years. Dr. David Sampson tells publicly of his family's most difficult Christmas years ago on the farm in Indiana. He was young and his mother died unexpectedly at a young age right before Christmas.

The family was in shock as Christmas approached. Death and sadness filled the air. Their tradition had always been that their dad would disappear from the house out there on the farm and go out looking for Santa on Christmas Eve and Dave's mom would stay with them in the house. While Dad was gone looking out in the countryside for Santa Claus, Santa himself would appear at the house, bearing gifts, climbing the roof to the house, and speaking down the chimney. The kids lived for that moment each year. Their father never found Santa, but Santa always appeared while Dad was out in the countryside looking for Santa. But they all knew this year was different.

But his dad did what he knew his wife would have wanted. He left the house on Christmas Eve to go search for Santa. As always, he never found Santa, but as always, while he was gone, Santa appeared fully dressed and full of Christmas cheer and greetings for a very happy little boy named David. The roof was climbed; gifts were delivered... the Story went on just as the mother wanted it to.

What a dad. What a Story. The Story cannot be crushed by anything, even Death. Dave learned that from his determined dad... his dad did what he knew he needed to... keep telling the Story of Saint Nicholas.

The Darkness will NOT overcome the Light. That is what John tells us. The Candle will not be extinguished by anything for those moms and dads who believe.

Oh, what a Story. Dave knew through his dad's actions that if Christmas happened that year then things were somehow going to be all right

Old, old Story. Candy canes were around long before us... created by the church to tell the Story. In 1670, the choirmaster at the Cologne Cathedral not far from here was faced with maintaining order among his young singers during the long Living Crèche ceremony. Wise in the ways of small children, be distributed among them sugar sticks to keep them quiet. In honor of the occasion, he had the candies bent into shepherds' crooks like those of the humble shepherds, first to worship the newborn Christ.

The candy canes shaped like shepherds' crooks became popular as part of the Living Crèche ceremonies all over northern Europe. In the early part of the last century, red and white became the colors of the candy cane and came to symbolize the Story of Christ... red representing the blood shed by Christ on the cross.

The Dutch of New York brought with them to the United States the love of Saint Nicolaas, a man who was born of wealthy parents in what is now Turkey in 271 A.D. He renounced his wealth, devoted himself to works of charity. He later became bishop and left a great legacy of what he did for the poor and needy.

Saint Nicholas is what this is all about. Pointing the way toward the Christ child and being generous to the world as Christ and Saint Nicholas were.

Pam's father said, concerning Santa Claus and candy canes and the Christian faith and all the discussion surrounding these aspects of our current Christmas celebration, in a sermon in Germany in December of 1987, "it all hangs together." Candy canes and shepherds' crooks, Saint Nicholas and Santa Claus, gifts and December 5th and December 25th... it all hangs together by the God who created it all... according to the gospel writer John.

Some worry about whether or not the kids "fully understand" the meaning of Christmas, fearing Santa will confuse the real meaning of Christmas. I say lead them to celebrate it fully each year and later in life they will sort out the Real Meaning. Celebrations will lead them, as it does many of us, to ponder the Real Meaning someday. For now, hug the Jolly Old Fellow.

I am 50 and just now starting to get it. No wonder I love Santa Claus and Sinta Klaus so much. My mom gave me the Story year after year, even those years in our lives growing up when I now know it was extremely challenging for her to gather the strength and resources to make Christmas happen for us.

I thanked her this year for the first time ever for always making Christmas so magical for us as kids. I just got it this year... here in northern Europe... where they celebrate Sinta Klaus Day on the day to honor Saint Nicholas. Mom even brought me into this world on Sinta Klaus' day, December 5th. No wonder I love him so... when you are born on a Saint's day, you may be forever tagged.

Remember the Story of David's dad? Many of us know someone this year that is facing Christmas without some loved one for the first time ever for them. Pray for them. David wrote of how difficult it must have been for his dad to make Christmas happen that year for his children. But he did.

David is now serving our country in D.C. I know of no one more compassionate, capable, and courageous than he to take on such tasks. With a mother's bright love that penetrated the Darkness and a father so determined to go find that Santa and to climb that roof when it would have been easier to sit in the darkness and mourn... well, such love and determination to celebrate Christmas is the kind of home from which guys like David come.

Gospel writer John says the Darkness cannot extinguish the Light. Celebrate.

And let's celebrate with this prayer of the Blessing of the Candy Canes as you hold your own candy cane just given to you by our children:

Blessings of the Candy Canes Prayer*

Let Us Pray,
Dear Lord, we give thanks for
Good Saint Nicholas, whom we remember
On this Feast Day
WE rejoice that he has been made
The Patron Saint
And the Holy Symbol of Joy
For many peoples of many lands.

155

We remember his generosity
As We, once again prepare our
Homes and hearts for the Great Feast
Of Christmas, the Birth of the
Eternal Blessing, Jesus Christ.
May these candy canes
Be a sign of advent joy for us.
May these candy canes
Shaped just like a bishop's staff
Be for us a sign of benevolence.
We rejoice that Saint Nicholas belongs to
The Great Fellowship of your
Saints across the centuries and
That his generosity has become a
Symbol that has delighted generations.
Help us to emulate Him, to be generous with
Our belongings, with our love, with
Ourselves.
May these candies carry with them, O Lord,
Your Bright Blessing.
May their sweet taste remind us of the Great
Sweetness of your Word on our tongues,
Your presence in our hearts.
Amen.

*Adapted from Prayers for the Domestic Church, by Edward
Hays, Forest of Peace Books, Inc.

Letter 24

Real Dutch
Christmas Tree

December 15, 2002

*It really is wonderful putting up
a Dutch Christmas Tree in your
living room while listening to
the melody and rhythm of
the church bells.*

John, or as we now call him, John the Baptist, was
born six months before Jesus and was the cousin of Jesus.
People of faith were eagerly and desperately awaiting the
promised birth of the Savior and some wondered if John,
born to Mary's cousin Elizabeth, was the One.

Thirty years later John was bearded, ate natural
foods, wore a loincloth, was part of a religious separatist
community that lived out in the desert, was a real hellfire-
and-brimstone preacher warning of the coming Judgment
Day, had a large following, and was baptizing hundreds in
the river Jordan, "Are YOU the Christ?" they asked?????"[1]

"Are you the REAL one?" they asked.

---

[1] John 1:19-28

There are two types of American families. One that believes in REAL Christmas trees and one that believes in ARTIFICIAL Christmas trees.

Military families are no different. Two groups... one that lugs its artificial tree around the world to every base and country and one that faces every obstacle in every country to get a real tree no matter what the cost in time, money, and energy.

Folks with artificial trees tend to be smug, I have noticed. They put a tree up in early November, saying all too smugly they do not have to worry about needles dropping or fire concerns from a dry tree. Takes them only 30 minutes to convert their living room into an artificial place of celebration. Tree goes up quickly and with no mess. Perfectly shaped trees.

One guy I knew, and he was a Baptist minister by the way, with a real bah-humbug spirit, proudly told of never taking his tree down... he simply dragged his fully-decorated artificial tree into the garage each December 26th morning and sat it in the corner of the garage with a black plastic garbage bag draped over it. The tree sat there in the garage all year long with ornaments on it.

One military chaplain, an Episcopal priest by the way, bought his artificial tree at a garage sale for $10, used it for 20+ years, finally got tired of his wife insisting on an artificial tree upgrade, so he tried to sell the tree for $5 at his own garage sale and could not... he stuck the whole tree into the ground in the yard of the house they rented... among the other little pine trees in the yard. It looked real. Rusted over the years, but still looked fairly real out there in the back yard.

We are a real tree family. Chevy Chase's Christmas Vacation opening movie scene is our family's inspiration. We love going out into the woods, like my own grandfather did on his farm in southern Ohio, selecting THE tree, cutting it down, and dragging it home.

Our daughter arrived yesterday at 10:00 a.m. at the Amsterdam airport. Came home, ate, and voted for us to get back into the car by 3:00 p.m. to go into the Dutch woods and "find 'er and cut 'er down." She had been traveling for over 24 hours from Auburn to Boerdonk, but she wanted to go on our annual family tree-hunting trip! Our house was all decorated 'cept for the tree. Amity wanted us to wait until she arrived for that part of the tradition. Always a good story in our family.

John, are you the REAL Savior or should we look for another? Looking for the REAL one is a part of the human need.

Pam is a "gatherer" in the family... she likes the social experience of looking for hours. Simply to look. She likes to LOOK at hundreds of trees. Amity and Daniel were cold... they were the "hunters"... find the tree quickly, kill it and chop it down, drag it out of the woods to the car and sling it on the roof. Amity says no need to look for the perfect one... just like in the movie Christmas Vacation, look for the one that you see the Light over... one that jumps out and says, "I AM THE ONE!"

Amity and Daniel looked at two trees sitting among hundreds, picked the second one within seconds, and that was it. Done. It was cold. Frigid. The Dutch are already ice-skating on the frozen canals. They never skated on the canals here last year. Not cold enough. And we froze last year. The Dutch said about the weather last winter with the fog, driving sleet, 5-hours-of-daylight' days, "Ah, this is real Dutch weather." This year, colder than ever and much earlier, they are saying, "OH, this is going to be harsh winter." Now a Dutch person using the word "harsh" has me concerned. We took the tree and ran. Amity said she saw the Light over the tree just like in Christmas Vacation.

As always, the tree looked better and fuller in the woods with all its little tree friends. Rather than struggle with getting it onto our car roof, we simply opened the tailgate, laid down the seats of our Durango, and shoved the tree in... all the way to the dashboard.

Problem began then. No Christmas tree stands to be found. Dutch don't have those little Wal-Mart metal bowls with the screws and legs to hold and balance the tree. The Dutch just nail two boards together in a cross, drive a nail up through the cross into the tree bottom, and set the thing down on the living room floor. No water, no bowl, no nothing. I could not even find two boards to make into a cross. Many Dutch put the REAL trees into their living room roots and all. Big ball of roots. We did that last year and the tree STILL died by January 6th, Epiphany Sunday. So we had to drag a dead REAL tree with roots through our house. No roots this year.

Finally found a huge Dutch hardware store with one Dutch version of the REAL Christmas tree stand. Could not believe it. It was a two-gallon bucket with a small plastic ring inside with a small, very small, hole in it to slip the tree through. I immediately asked how the tree is supposed to stay up... simple Dutch answer. Stick the tree in and fill the bucket with many, many rocks... to the top.

Got the tree and plastic bucket home and looked immediately to see where I could attach wires to the ceiling to hold the tree up... no place to attach wires to hold the top of the tree. This was a challenge... there would be no wires. Had to spend a couple of hours finding my axe and hand-saw still packed in boxes in the garage and whittling down the trunk of the tree so that it would even FIT into the bucket. Had Pam holding the tree up in the bucket while I placed rock after rock after rock into the bucket. Cleaned out every large white garden rock Daniel could find to pile around the bottom of the tall tree... it was bumping against our ceiling. Our 1916 Dutch farmhouse has high ceilings.

One American family here believes in artificial trees... November 1st theirs goes up.

I had to trim away branches from the bottom of our tree so that I could pile rocks high enough to hold it upright. Top-heavy trees take a lot of rocks to hold them up. Kids call it our "nature tree." We have a real tree and real rocks to hold it up. Real Dutch deal. Pam's handmade tree-skirt, rather large around and usually covering the floor beneath the tree, now covers the rocks... draping perpendicular to the ground draped over the pile of rocks.

Only took 6 hours to get the tree to stand on its own. We were all exhausted from sawing, holding the tree, and carrying rocks into our living room. No squirrels jumped out, unlike in the movie Christmas Vacation with Chevy Chase... chasing around a squirrel who came in with the REAL tree from the woods!

But we have a REAL tree. Our Christmas tree stand is in storage back in the States... had no idea what a mistake that was to leave it there. I will throw away tree and Dutch bucket stand and all on January 6th and have some caring family member send me a Wal-Mart stand from the States next year.

But we have a real tree standing (leaning actually) precariously upright in our living room. I called Shawn Kitchin to rub it in... he believes in fake trees, has had his up since November 1st. No natural smell. No fun stories. Only thing he keeps saying is, "Well, I got mine up before you got yours up." He's so competitive.

John said he is not the REAL savior. It is Jesus, the One whose shoes John is not worthy to tie. John is just here to point the Way to that Jesus. May we find the Real Messiah among all the artificiality of the Season as it all, like John, points us toward the Messiah.

I called Shawn at 10:00 p.m. and told him of the Dutch tree stand story and that it took 6 hours to whittle the tree, locate a bucket, carry in the rocks, pile them around the base of the tree, etc. Big job with no tree stand.

He said, "Should have asked. I have a nice tree stand from Wal-Mart in my garage. Don't need it. You could have used mine and saved a lot of time."

Man, I hate people who believe in artificial trees. They are so smug.

Gotta go home and put some more rocks around our tree. It was leaning this morning from the weight of the ornaments. There is a lot of weight from 27 years worth of keepsake ornaments. Lots to celebrate. It is wonderful to celebrate communion with you this Advent Sunday. Amen.

Dutch Fog

December 22, 2002

Though the fog prevents us from seeing much of the village and the church, the bells continue to ring in Boerdonk, letting us know the church is still there.

One year ago Pam and I would get headaches just trying to drive through the fog to the local Dutch grocery to get some milk. It was too foggy, we would get too lost, and we dreaded even needing milk. It took much effort to navigate in the fog. It was extremely foggy ALL the time here last winter. Dark, foggy, and easy to get lost. The roads do not go east or west or north or south... they zigzag every direction. Trying to find the sun for directional help was useless. There was no sun in the fog.

Talk about a fog. Mary was trying to get some sleep. She was nauseous. Sleep was elusive. Pregnant. Not what she wanted. Some voice enters her head and tells her to "not be afraid. God is with you." Fog is confusing.

Joseph found out she was with child, and he was a bit restless. Could not sleep. Had a headache. The public expected him to have her stoned to death per the law of the day for being engaged to him and for becoming pregnant. Same voice tells him (paraphrased by me), "Do not be afraid. God is in control of all this." Relax and let me lead you through the fog.[1]

Right.

Everyone has stories of getting lost in the Dutch fog. We all get so sick of being lost in the fog over here. You can be within ten minutes of home, get lost in a thick fog, and not get home for hours.

Sermons and worship are God's attempt to help you either navigate in the fog of life or to help you at least relax a bit when you are lost in the fog.

Last week this pastor apparently touched on a nerve in every home. Preaching on the topic of REAL Christmas trees versus artificial trees is obviously an issue in most every home. Apparently, America is full of funny Christmas Tree stories.

General Peyton Cole wrote of how his wife kept after him in Michigan to take the family and go out into the woods and cut THE tree. Frigid cold, heavy parkas... the whole Chevy Chase Christmas Vacation scene. Every tree was acceptable to all members of the family 'cept young Peyton Cole III. No tree was acceptable. Finally Father Cole was so frustrated he let out a sentence of expletives and asked the crying little Peyton, "WHAT in the world do you WANT in a tree?" "I want one with lights on it!" the young child cried back!

The fog of family life.

Robert Hamilton, retired Navy pilot, told of the tree he cut and dragged into the living room one year that could

[1] Matthew 1:18-25

not be positioned to the point of being acceptable. His wife finally told him she would rather not have a tree than have a crooked tree in the house. He said "Fine," and took the tree down and threw it out on the street. Neighbor came by and asked if she could have the tree. "Sure," Robert said. Neighbor took the tree home, cut it in two, eliminating the bent part of the trunk, and had a beautifully straight tree for nothing. The Hamilton family has been an artificial tree family ever since.

Phil Garrant told of the year in Massachusetts when he went out to cut his real tree. An annoying vine was wrapped around the trunk of the tree which he had to remove with great effort. Next day he was covered from head to foot with a severe case of poison ivy. One guy told me his father back in the States keeps his artificial tree up and decorated in the family living room the entire year... says the tree is beautiful, and it makes the house feel like Christmas year around.

Brian Neyedli from Canada sent me a cartoon. A man is pummeled with all the activity of Christmas... shopping, sales, cards, malls, tree-shopping. Finally goes into a church with stained glass and just sits... tells the pastor he came into the church to get away from Christmas. Great cartoon. We all can identify with that need for some Silent Night.

Karen White, an Air Force attorney, wrote and "admitted" she was an artificial tree person. I admitted back that we had one REAL tree and two artificial trees in our house. Confession is good for the soul.

Mary, don't be afraid. Joseph, don't be afraid. This all has meaning. I will help you through the fog.

In the movie Home Alone, there is a wonderful scene on Christmas Eve when the scary old neighbor and the young scared boy named Kevin accidentally meet at the church. Just the man and the boy and the children's choir. The old man tells the young boy, "Don't believe all the bad things you have heard about me. I will not harm you." The boy is in church because he is scared and abandoned, and the man is in church because he is estranged from his son and granddaughter and is trying to get reconnected to them.

We love watching that movie, and I love that scene. A scared abandoned boy at church and an old man who scares people trying to get reconnected to his family. They had all made some mistakes. The scene reminds me of God telling us "Don't believe all the bad things you have heard about Me. I will not harm you."

Christmas is a fun time of the year to get reconnected. Chris and Becky Henz were in my college class I taught as a seminary student 20 years ago in Fort Worth, Texas. We lost track of each other over the years. I got an email from the Middle East last week from an Air Force chaplain assistant deployed there. She had been forwarded an email from her home base in Massachusetts that Chris had sent in October. Chris had contacted her via the web page the Chief of Chaplain's office this fall to try and locate me... they told him I was stationed at Hanscom Air Force base. I had been... two assignments ago. THAT makes one feel good. He emailed Tracy at Hanscom, she accessed her email in the Middle East on her deployment, and she forwarded on the search information to me which included Chris' phone number. I called Chris at Motorola in Fort Worth... he got his wife on the phone immediately on a 3-way call and said, "Hey, Honey, you owe me $10... I found Gary and Pam first."

Glad to bond families together through such bets. Made us feel good to know families were betting on us.

Here in Boerdonk Pam and I hosted a Christmas Open House this week. I knew many Americans were looking forward to playing ping-pong at our house, but Pam prevailed. She served all her food ON the table. Great serving table. Tom Kirkham walked in, saw the food covering the ping-pong table, and said to his wife Susan, "Honey, I owe you

$10." He had bet I would not allow Pam to use the table for the party. His wife, a good Texas hostess and sensing a sure bet, tried to tell him this was an OPEN HOUSE and that there would NOT be any ping-pong.

Keeping another family together through betting... isn't life wonderful? So many fun stories around Christmas. Wonderful time of the year.

Last night I told Shawn and Pam Kitchin that I would take them and Shawn's mother to the castle not too far from here. They followed our family through the fog. Fog doesn't scare me anymore in Holland. No more headaches. Getting lost does not bother me anymore. Happens all the time. I get speeding tickets now I am so comfortable.

Heavy fog last night. Got lost. Never got a headache. Never found the castle. Drove through the same village three times. Pam said all three times to turn left. I turned right all three times. Fog in the family.

And we don't worry about where to buy milk in the Dutch fog anymore. Found out the village grocer, who lived across the street from us the whole time and we never knew it, delivers milk TO our neighborhood twice a week. Delivers it to us in person. And we did not know.

We never could find or figure out God over the centuries. So He came to us in the fog... in a Manger. He came to us. In the fog. We could not find Him, so He came for us. In person. And told us to "not be afraid."

Relax in the fog this week. We have much to celebrate. Join us Tuesday night at 5:00 p.m. at the Venhorst Church for the Christmas Eve Service. Go to Boekel and turn right. Or call Pam and ask for directions. Enjoy your drive through the fog. Amen

Letter 26

Losing at Monopoly

January 5, 2003

*I wondered yesterday if the village leaders would
allow me to ring the church bells in celebration of
the Auburn football win over Penn State!*

A football report from Boerdonk.

Underdog #19-ranked Auburn upset #9-ranked Penn State 13-9 on January 1st and Underdog #2-ranked Ohio State upset #1-ranked Miami University 31-24 in double overtime Friday night. Being part owner and financial supporter of the Auburn football team via tuition payments and, having grown up in the Buckeye State of Ohio, the year is starting out great for this chaplain.

The only thing better would have been to start the New Year with a win at Monopoly.

Not only is it the first Sunday of the New Year, it is also Epiphany Sunday. A parishioner asked this past week what the word "Epiphany" means... love being asked such questions. Finally get to use some of that seminary training of 20 years ago. Same parishioner asks me regularly why they do not give voice lessons in seminary to men and women training to be pastors.

Epiphany means "an appearance or manifestation of a god or other supernatural being" and "a yearly Christian festival held on January 6th commemorating the revealing of Jesus as the Christ to the Gentiles in the persons of the Magi" (wise men traveling from afar... or perhaps the three Texans dressed in firemen suits heading to a Christmas costume party claiming they are "coming from a far" (fire – some Texans pronounce the word "fire" as "far") at Bethlehem: also called the Twelfth Night.

Epiphany, January 6th, is the Twelfth Day after Christmas. Took the wise men some time to travel and follow the star and arrive at the manger.[1]

The Christmas Story goes on after Christmas. Long after the sales and no matter what the consumer tradition and market say.

Our live tree has not dropped any needles and is still standing in our living room. It will come down after January 6th. It is so alive we are concerned it may have rooted THROUGH our living room floor.

The Story keeps going. A few thousand years before Christ was born, the writer Isaiah said that folks would come bearing gifts of gold and frankincense and proclaiming the praises of the Lord.

It happened when the Wise Men went to the manger that sat below the Star. The Story was going on.

The song goes on. As your pastor, it is my privilege to be in your homes and lives. Some of you tell and show me more than any pastor wants to know. "Overshare" as some of you call it. The Magi got front row seats in seeing the newborn Savior. As your pastor, I get a front row seat to watch how God works in your family life.

---

[1] Mark 1:7-11

The lives of your families are an Epiphany for me some days.

Burnt or undercooked meals. Late to church. Family arguments. Parenting blunders. Sending children and money to college back in the States while serving your country during these times over here. Laughter. Disappointments. Hope. Loyalty.

A woman in one church one year told of how she grew up in a single-parent home with her father who had to work all the time to support her as an only child. No mother around to model mothering, to teach cooking, to sit with in church. No father around to provide special times with... life was too hard just trying to get food on the table.

The girl has turned into a model mother and parent. The church saved her, sustains her, and is the center of her life for her and her family. Laughter and Hope fill the home along with lots of very human and godly moments.

How does THAT work? Or what is THAT all about? How does she come from THAT home and become the mother, wife, church leader, and friend that she is? How does THAT happen?

God. The Story goes on and on. The Christmas Story goes on in spite of the mistakes we parents make. God is God.

We can just do our best and let God do the rest. As parents, as Air Force folks, as humans.

The one thing I wanted to do this year before Amity got back on the plane to return to Auburn was to play Monopoly on January 1st. She used to love to play Monopoly as a little girl, and I was often too busy as a dad to play with her. Monopoly took so much time, and I had too many very important Air Force things to do. At least that is what I believed at the time. Amity would ask me to play, and I would give that dreadful parent's answer "maybe tomorrow."

One day I peeked into her bedroom to say "good-bye" to her as I was going out the door, and she was playing Monopoly on the floor... by herself. Ripped my heart out. Pam joined her on the floor, and I left... to go save the world or some dumb thing like that.

My cousin Debbie taught me to play Monopoly back in the early 60's. My mother had divorced and had to move us kids back into the grandparent's house on the farm in southern Ohio. We had lived in a nice house in the city with running water and now moved to the farm with no running water. My cousins lived with the grandparents also because my Aunt Anna had divorced and she and her two daughters had moved back onto the farm also. It was wonderful for me. I loved being with all the cousins... ALL the time, in that three-bedroom house with no running water. I got to use a bucket to help Grandpa draw water out of the cistern well each morning, to light the wood in the woodstove to provide heat and hot water for the day everyday including summer days, and to use the outhouse in the middle of the cold nights. Picked out a live chicken on Sundays for the after-church dinner Grandma cooked for the preacher and his wife.

It was a big ongoing family reunion... everyday. And Debbie, the oldest cousin, taught us all how to play Monopoly. The game took hours and she always won. My dream was to beat Debbie someday. With no TV stations that worked, Monopoly filled lots of hours. Debbie and Monopoly taught Connie and me math, banking, strategy, patience, and luck. Taught us to cheat also... we got so tired of losing we united forces, cheated... and still lost. Debbie used to laugh hard as she piled her money in a basket.

We bought a Monopoly game last year, but never played. This year we played on January 1st. We were selecting what we were going to be in the game. Amity wanted the dog. Mom wanted the horse. Daniel wanted the car.

I said, "I will take the boot because I am going to kick all of your behinds today." Much to my surprise, Amity laughed hard and said, "You ALWAYS used to take the boot. You ALWAYS say the same thing... that you are going to kick our behinds in Monopoly."

Grace. Epiphany. She remembered playing so many games with me that she remembered such comments. I had one memory of her playing alone, and she had other memories.

We loaned each other money so the game would go on. No one seemed to want it to end.

My mom keeps apologizing for such rough days we had as kids when things did not go so well, and we had to move back to the farm. She has one memory, and I have another. What she thinks she has to keep apologizing for are some of my best memories. I still cherish those Monopoly memories with my cousins Debbie and Connie.

Young weekend seminarians from Asbury Seminary in northern Kentucky would drive across the Ohio River each weekend and serve poor small churches in southern Ohio. Debbie and Connie never missed their youth meetings. Debbie went to Asbury, has a degree in counseling, is married to a Methodist pastor, and served as a missionary while at Asbury. Connie, a teacher, is married to Ross, a banker. They are active in their church in Florida, and their daughter Brooke surprised them by being the Scripture Reader at the University Church she attends as a college student. I was able to have a wonderful reunion with Debbie this past fall in Ohio and received a Christmas card from the teacher, Mrs. Thompson, who taught Debbie, Connie, and me in the fourth and fifth grades. She loved us; made us laugh, loved teaching, and prayed for us. Strong woman of faith. Was able to see her this fall in Ohio... first time since 1964. The Story goes on.

We do our best, and God does the rest.

I lost the Monopoly game. Daniel and Amity had piles of money and laughed just like Debbie used to. But there are many more important things in life than winning, right? THAT is an Epiphany for some of us, huh?

Can't wait to beat many of you in ping-pong and golf this year... to keep you humble. That is my calling as your pastor. Happy New Year. Go do your best... and let God do the rest.

Letter 27

Boerdonk Bonfire in January

January 12, 2003

With Arctic cold threatening to freeze us all, the church bell sounds sliced through the air like and ice breaker forcing its way through solid seas.

It is frigid in Boerdonk today.

Mark writes "In those days...."[1]

Yesterday was the coldest it has been in seven years, say the locals. We had just taken down our Christmas tree, and it lay frozen out in the snow and the near-zero temperatures. Birds have fought around the bird feeder in our back yard for the seed, peanuts, and bread we offer each morning to them. Too cold to be outside.

Saturday morning was going to be so relaxing and cozy, staying indoors and sleeping in our warm Dutch

---

[1] Matthew 2:1-12

farmhouse. Those steam radiators... heat-a-rators as one young astute American calls them - make it comfortable to hibernate here in northern Europe on weekends. Nothing happens on these January days in Boerdonk.

At 7:00 a.m. on a normally quiet, frozen Saturday morning here in Boerdonk, with only church bells ringing, there was suddenly lots of noise with children laughing, talking, and pulling noisy wooden wagons around the village. Jumped from my bed to see what the matter was.

As always, this obviously was something else happening in our Boerdonk lives that we did not understand. Everybody else knew something we did not know. Happens daily when you are a foreigner and the rituals, customs, and routines are not known to you.

You sit and watch and wonder out your sleeping room window... wondering what you are missing.

Mark writes "In those days...."

We wondered what was happening in Boerdonk this early Saturday morning.

Kids were dragging Christmas trees down the street. Pam wanted to know what in the world was going on out our window... no one in Boerdonk ever makes noise early on a frigid Saturday morning. Our sleeping room window is right on the Boerdonk brick street... bricks and wooden wagon wheels make lots of noise... so much noise you could barely hear Baloo bark. And that is a lot of noise.

I told Pam kids were hauling trees... dead Christmas trees... down the street. Kids on bikes were dragging trees. Kids were walking carrying trees. A tractor rode by our sleeping room window slowly... trees were piled high on the wagon. Baloo was upset.

Nice quiet January Saturday morning in Boerdonk. Pam mumbled "Oh, THAT is what that paper flyer was telling us about." Not reading Dutch pretty much keeps us in the dark in Boerdonk.

Hours later when the grocery truck came in front of our house and honked, I finally braved the cold. I love going shopping at the grocery truck. Push a button and the hydraulic door opens for you. Sander the grocery man always greets you warmly with a smile and humor for the day. Villagers gather to buy groceries for the week and visit.

The grocery truck is where I get to find out what in the world is going on in Boerdonk that we do not have a clue about... which is a weekly occurrence.

Found out two important pieces of information. Johnny, Sander's assistant, asked where our dog Baloo was. Johnny always places grocery advertisements through the mail slot in our door that is near floor height... and Baloo always ferociously attacks the mail slot, trying to bite Johnny's hand and eating the paper flyers at the same time. Pam is so embarrassed that she catches and locks Baloo up when the grocery truck appears. I told Johnny that Baloo was locked up to save Johnny's hand. He said he missed having Baloo eat the mail yesterday and added, "It is cool that such a dog eats mail. It is my excitement for the week in Boerdonk. Nothing else happens here. I look forward to the dog making my life exciting."

I had fun telling Pam that Baloo IS the excitement for the week in Boerdonk and the topic of conversation at the grocery truck.

Secondly, I found out that the Saturday after Epiphany Day is the Day of the Burning of the Christmas Trees in Boerdonk and other surrounding villages in Holland. The kids ask, through their flyer we threw away without

177

understanding, that you place your dead Christmas tree in front of your house, and they pick it up.

"Where do they put them all?" I asked. WHAT is happening here??????

Sander had a cute Dutch girl explain it all to me. They were piling the trees behind the church and there would be a huge bonfire at 6:30 p.m. that night. Whole village would be there. It happens every year.

They came and picked up our tree. We attended the Burning of the Christmas Trees last night. Whole village was there. Fire Department from closest city came to oversee the event. Tent was set up for hot drinks. Huge bonfire.

The Boerdonk Church Youth Group organizes this each year in Boerdonk. Funny thing was, as I told a villager last night and she laughed hard, is that last year our tree laid in our back yard until June... trash company in Holland will not take trees, and we had no idea how to get rid of the darned thing. Finally a neighbor offered to haul it to the dump for me in June.

Saturday after Epiphany Sunday is the day the Church Youth Group gathers the community together to watch all the Christmas trees go up in flames.

Sunday after Epiphany Sunday is the day we all gather to remember the Baptism of The Lord and to remember our own Baptism. To remember who we are. Folks of Boerdonk always know what days to do what... they learn it growing up. Today is the day we Christians come to the altar and have water put on our heads in the form of a cross... to remember who we are and Whose we are. To remind ourselves of how we are to live.

When things in life would get discouraging or self-doubt would threaten, Martin Luther used to repeat over and over again to himself, "I am baptized. I am baptized."

It does make a difference to be baptized. And it does help to remind yourself, "I am baptized." Norman Johnson, a dear friend with whom we worshipped at the Hanscom chapel, used to comment to me that this Baptism of the Lord Sunday service was his favorite service of the year. Many of us like to be reminded Whose we are by having the cross marked on our forehead with water.

Yesterday was the day to burn trees. Today is the day to have water marked on your head.

And it happened in those days that Jesus came from Nazareth of Galilee and was baptized by John in the river Jordan. Details of daily life were important to the writer Mark... city, river name, name of John... it all happened in "those days." Let it all happen in these days where you live, buy groceries, burn trees, and are awakened early on Saturday mornings by laughing village kids. God was there at the River Jordan, and He is here in Boerdonk, Kalkar, Volkel, and Kleine Brogul. In these days. Remind yourself... and then face the week. It does make a difference that you are baptized. In these days especially. Amen.

Letter 28

"I'm Glad I Don't Have a TV"

January 26, 2003

One wonders if the church bells must have heaters somewhere near them in the steeple. It is SO cold here in Boerdonk.

This morning's reading was from the book of the prophet Jonah. Prophets warn folks of what is to come.

If you are a Christian who follows the Christian church calendar, today is the Third Sunday in Ordinary Time. Ordinary time is that time between Christmas/Epiphany and Lent/Easter. Just normal time. Just another Sunday.

If you are an American Christian, today is Super Bowl Sunday. NOT just another Sunday.

The Super Bowl will start at 1:00 a.m. tonight here in Europe. Some would give anything to have a prophet tell them who will win the game tonight. Tell us the future.

Jonah was a Prophet. You know the Jonah story.[1] He was not a cooperative prophet. God wanted him to go to the city of Nineveh and tell the folks that if they did not repent and straighten up he was going to destroy them and their whole city. Jonah wanted nothing to do with being the one to take that message to those people, so he went fishing on a boat, heading AWAY from Nineveh.

Storm came up, men on board got scared, wanted to know who was causing the storm. Back in those days when things went wrong, folks figured someone had angered God. They drew straws to find out the culprit. Jonah's short straw indicated he was the problem, so they threw him overboard. To die. Huge fish swallowed him. Lived through the fish mucus and dodged digestive processes down there, and the fish finally got so sick from food that would not digest that he spit Jonah up... onto the beach. Jonah's actions even made the fish sick.

God was a determined parent who cared both for the people of Nineveh and for Jonah.

Now Jonah is again told, "Go to the great city of Nineveh, and tell them I will destroy them if they do not repent." Jonah went there this time. He was tired of being fish food.

Jonah went to tell them they were going to be destroyed in forty days. Forty days is an important period of time in the Bible. Jesus fasted for forty days in the desert. Jonah preached and waited to watch the fireworks... God was going to wipe out the whole city.

Jonah was mad for being made to go to Nineveh, but he seemed to enjoy telling fellow human beings their Creator was going to destroy them. God the Father was angry and

---

[1] Jonah 1:1-4:11

was threatening to take them off the planet. Things were about to get ugly.

Being family and raising children and being kids are not easy. God is not pleased; Jonah is wondering how in the world he ever got involved in all this, and the people of Nineveh are clueless and merrily going about their business.

This story has some routine daily life stuff in it. There is some anger, some parenting threats, some humor with the fish eating Jonah, some anticipation concerning God's threatened destruction of Nineveh. Lots of twists in the story, similar to the twists in our daily walk with God in life, huh?

Jonah goes throughout a very large city screaming to anyone who would listen that they all were about to be destroyed.

When our kids were much younger, we were having a "family discussion" early on a Saturday morning. Amity loved to watch cartoons on Saturday and I, as a good threatening parent, was not above using her love for TV as leverage in parenting. She had a TV in her bedroom and she loved that TV... and loved its being in her bedroom.

Some incident happened — don't even remember the particulars – and Amity was not doing what I asked. I asked repeatedly. To no avail.

Finally, I threatened with the threat of threats. If she did not obey, I would march into that room and remove the TV. And I did. I had warned her.

She really got upset with me. I disconnected the TV, carried it through the living room into the storage room with the cord dangling and dragging along behind it. Amity was screaming and pleading with me to please put the TV back in her room... it was not a pleasant experience for either of us. It was never going into her room again I exclaimed.

Daniel, about four years old, watched the whole thing in silence from the patio with his face pressed against the door glass. Not a peep. After the TV was stored and locked in storage and Amity marched back to her room to never speak to me again, there was a silence.

Daniel looked at me and said, "Boy, I am glad I don't have a TV."

No TV means one less thing Dad can take from me. One less thing Dad can punish me with... less leverage if there is no TV. Family life is so funny. And so fun. By the end of the morning, we were all laughing over that line. She corrected her actions, TV was put back into her room, dinner was served, and we all ate at the table. Parents were at least temporarily being obeyed.

The people of Nineveh repented. Bible says that even God repented. You won't hear that being said much in the Bible. God repented of the evil He had threatened to do to the people He loved. Even God repented.

Jonah? He was mad. He had gone through a lot with being swallowed by a fish and all. And now God was not going to destroy them? Jonah went off and pouted under a tree.

What can we learn from this story of Jonah?

Some days we are the disobeying and uncooperative Jonah, running from God. Some days we are the guys fishing on the boat... we will throw anybody into the sea to the fish just to get rid of the storm and have peace and to save ourselves. Some days we are like the threatening God. Some days we are the people of Nineveh and need to just repent.

Some days we are the prophet Jonah who is doing great things for God. Some days we are the prophet Jonah who is simply fish food at the moment. Nothing more. Nothing less. Just fish food. Some days we are simply eaten up by people or situations. Then spit out.

And some days we are like God our Creator who threatens and then we change our minds. Some days I am the Loving Parent who cares enough for my child that I take away her TV, threatening to never return it.

And then I give it back. She repented, and I repented and gave back the TV.

God loves you. He loves you just the way you are but too much to let you stay that way. Bow your beads, and tell God you repent. Then, according to Jonah, God will repent and not do the threatening things you have heard he will do.

What can we learn? That parents need to repent some times. That children need to repent. That prophets and chaplains are very human... some days good prophets, other days just fish food. Even the fish get sick of us. And that God is in all of this... emotions, threats, and all. That we are loved so much by God that even after making threats He will later repent. And that we need to laugh. Above all else. Laugh. And eat together in the evenings after all is said and done. That Love for each other overcomes all.

Enjoy watching your TV tonight. You heard it first from your chaplain. Fish stories and Tampa Bay go together. Go Tampa Bay. I love being a part of this family called the Family of God. Go Tampa Bay.

Letter 29

Dutch Solace

February 23, 2003

*We find the church bells
so consoling some days.*

Today is the Seventh Sunday in Ordinary Time. One more Sunday of Ordinary Time and then Carnival is upon us just before Ash Wednesday and then six weeks of Lent. But today is an Ordinary Day. Color is green. No green in this part of the world in February, but green is the church color nonetheless. The earth is bare, color is brown, it is cold, and the sun rarely shines. It is just winter in northern Europe. Another ordinary European winter day.

But the Scripture reading this morning is anything but ordinary. If you can get your head around it, it is not only an incredible story at many levels, but it is very funny with lots of surprises. Not an ordinary day for some folks.

Jesus returned to Capernaum, probably hoping to spend some quiet time at home.[1] He often liked to get away from the crowds to pray and re-create. "It became known he was home." Understatement. Word spread Jesus was in

---

[1] Mark 2: 1-12

the house and such a large crowd gathered, there was no longer any room for them, not even around the door.

He is preaching and someone needs a doctor. Four guys carry a very sick man, a paralytic, on a mat (cot), fighting the crowd all the way. They can't get through to Jesus, so they climb on the roof.

With the guy. Can you imagine what the guy on the cot is thinking? "Hey, put me down, I am sick enough as it is. Hey, don't drop me from the roof! Hey, what the heck are you guys doing???????"

They get the cot and the sick guy on the roof, tell the guy to trust them, and proceed to rip the roof off the house. They are going to drop in on Jesus, so to speak. "After they had broken through, they let the mat down."

Now that is a memorable scene while preaching. Roof being ripped off, Jesus preaching away, some guy falls out of the sky, Jesus is startled, looks up, and sees four friends grinning. They wave and point to their friend. Heal him, they ask.

Instead of healing the man, Jesus says, "Your sins are forgiven." Typical preacher. Dealing with spiritual things instead of worldly things. They are typical parishioners. They are not listening to His sermon, they just want their needs met. They want their friend healed. They want him to feel better and to function in life. Preacher's interests and people's needs often miss connecting in church or in home.

Jesus is not having a quiet day at home.

And then you have the self-appointed "preacher monitors" of the church in this story. They accuse Jesus immediately of blasphemy for offering forgiveness. They sat around waiting for one wrong word to come out of Jesus' mouth. They then pounce. Some churches, usually ones not doing so well, have such critics who dominate the church. They judge, but not much else. They did not help carry the guy in, they did not help take the roof off, and their job as they saw it was to simply criticize any "wrong" word Jesus spoke. As soon as Jesus told the guy his sins were forgiven, they spoke out and claimed Jesus was blaspheming God... only God can forgive sins they said. They did not take note that the four friends had gone to a lot of effort to get the sick guy to Jesus, they did not take note that the roof of the house was now ruined, they did not take note of the gathered crowd... they were just there to criticize.

Three men from Kalkar in Germany needed some serious counseling yesterday. Let's call them Mike Cronin, Dean Nilson, and Vinny just for the sake of this story. The sun was shining (a rare thing in February in northern Europe), and the sky was clear and deceptively looking a bit like spring. These three boys called their pastor and asked this chaplain to drive two hours round trip to Germany and play golf on a Saturday afternoon.

There is nothing more relaxing for me than to play golf on a beautiful German course. Not much more of a scenic view than to be standing on the fairway wondering what to shoot for and to be told "Just hit it toward that windmill." We had a dinner to attend Saturday night in Eindhoven at Daniel's International School (potluck dinner with food brought by 200 families from 43 different nations), but there was time to go do some "counseling" with Mike, Dean, and Vinny prior to the potluck dinner.

Typical preacher. Give me a day with golf and a potluck dinner, and I am in heaven.

Loaded up my black bag with 13 clubs, balls, tees, gloves, shoes, etc. into the car. I won that bag nearly 20 years ago at a two-person-team tournament at Carswell Air Force Base. My partner, Chaplain Tom Bush, and I were tied for the tournament lead, and this was the playoff hole. It was a 200-yard par three up hill... above a valley. I teed off and drove the ball over the green into the rough on the backside of the green on the playoff hole. Now we were looking at an impossible downhill chip onto a steeply sloped green, with three hills on the huge green between our ball and the hole. Impossible to chip the ball and to hold the green. Tom chipped and his ball hit the green above the hole and shot past the hole down the hill into the valley below the hole. We were dead. I pulled out my putter... not going to try a chip shot. Tom always laughed at me for using my putter off the green.

I putted. The ball rolled out of the rough, over three hills, down the slope, hit the flag, and dropped into the hole. We each won a beautiful black bag that weighs a ton. Caddy killers, they are called. Tom quit laughing at me for using that putter off the green.

So my huge bag and I arrived at the German course for some relaxation yesterday.

Things deteriorated from there. I was about to get an education on German golf rules.

Winter rules they call them. No carts to drive. I like to drive a cart when possible... bad knees and Caddy killer bag much too heavy to carry. Bag is as big as I am. So I asked to rent a pull cart for my bags. No pull carts allowed during the winter.

I can't carry that huge bag of clubs around. THAT is NOT a relaxing afternoon. Plus I have to get back home to attend a potluck dinner and prepare a sermon. Have to have some energy left at the end of the day!

Asked how much the cute little bags were there in the golf shop... lightweight ones for carrying. The German lady was overwhelmed with the unusually large February crowd and could not determine the price of the bag. And we had only four minutes until our tee time... if we missed it, we would lose our place on the course.

Like the guys ripping off the roof to get their friend to Jesus, sometimes you have to adjust your plans in life.

I rushed to the car, threw the bag into the trunk, and kept only four "sticks." My 5-wood, putter, 7-iron, and pitching wedge.

Grabbed another sweater also. It was colder than the blue sky and sun made it look.

Ran back to the first tee. They made fun of me for only having four sticks to swing. I told them I have fewer choices to make. Keeps life simple.

Then I made fun of them for using little plastic cups as tees... told them I would buy them some tees next time so they could be real men on the course. Little plastic cup tees... what wimps.

They all hit ahead of me. I went to the box and tried to stick my wooden tee... a man's tee... into the ground. The tee snapped. Second German winter rule. Use plastic cups for your ball... ground is frozen solid. (As Mark Blake says, "We're not in Mississippi anymore.") Tee will not go into the frozen tundra. Not one bit. The other three guys started laughing... now I had only four clubs and a pocket full of useless wooden tees.

Mike asked me if I wanted to use any of his new "floating balls" cause there is a lot of water on this course. Told him I did not plan to need them because I did not plan to hit any of my shots into the water.

Third hole had lots of water. My tee shot strayed left and went out of view... Mike said there was water over there where we could not see. His shot followed mine.

He was wrong. There was not water there. My ball and his were sitting on TOP of the water... his expensive floating ball and my non-floating ball. They were sitting there with several other errant shots... sitting on the ice. Solid ice. He said he guessed he did not need the floating golf balls today. It drove me crazy seeing all those balls sitting out there on the ice for the picking... except we could not get them... ice was too thin. Some days I would just as soon have fun finding good golf balls on the course as score well. I was drooling, eyeing those balls sitting on the ice.

I almost went home. I am a fair weather golfer. I am hand carrying four sticks, can't get my tees into the frozen ground, and ice on every hole. They even told me it is a REQUIREMENT in Germany to use a tee on the fairway in the winter... so as to not hurt the dormant grass.

But I was determined to play golf no matter how much adjustment was required. Those four guys were so determined to get their friend to Jesus that they adjusted, took off a roof, ignored the sermon, trumped the crowd, interrupted the service, and dropped their friend into Jesus' lap. And listened to the arguing between Jesus and the preacher monitors. Nothing deterred them. They wanted their friend healed. Period.

Jesus forgave the guy his sins, healed him, and told him to go out and tell the church, the priests, and the world what great things had happened. No, Jesus did not do that. He forgave the guy, healed him, and told him to go back home. The guy picked up his mat (I love that part also... he did not want to give up his mat and I don't want to give up my old black Caddy-killer bag... we all have favorite things we cling to in life) and left.

They all said they had never seen anything like what they had just seen. What a day. Go call the roof repairman.

Go home, Jesus told the man. Go home and recover. Being healed is an exhausting thing with the roof deal and all.

Home is where our hearts and minds can be healed from the pain of life, is it not?

Valentine's Day, February 14, 2003. Our landlord and his wife came over to our home in the late afternoon. Dutch don't visit much during the winter — that is saved more for the summer. So it was unusual for them to come to our door. They stood there with beautiful red roses for Pam, candy for Daniel, and a cake. Came in with some obvious intention to stay. Pam offered them coffee. They accepted. Sat down on the couch. We knew something was on their minds but could not tell what. He kept glancing at his watch.

He has his own TV, but at a certain time he asked us if we were going to watch TV. Then we began to figure out why they were in our home. The United Nations Security Council was being briefed that day concerning Iraq. Our landlord settled in for a couple of hours.

They came to sit with us. Just to sit with us and watch the UN briefing. We had heard Dutch families had gone into American homes and sat with them on September 11th. Every American family had been "covered" with a home visit by a Dutch family on September 11, 2001 immediately after the terrorist bombings in the United States. The Dutch consoled and provided solace as only they can do. With presence in your living room. Not one American family was left unvisited.

Toon and Anne came just to sit with us. Toon began to tell us stories he had not shared with us before. He told us of May 10, 1940. That was the day the Germans occupied Holland. He worked in the café as a young teenage boy here in Boerdonk when the Occupation happened. He shook his head. He told us of September 1944 when American parachutes filled the skies over Boerdonk... and many of them were shot while in their parachutes in the skies as the Dutch looked on in horror and in hopefulness that enough Americans would survive to free the Dutch.

He came to sit with Pam, Daniel, and me. Just to sit. He teased our little dog, and our dog nipped him. He said, "Ah, typical American dog." I reminded him the dog was from Belgium. He laughed. There is no lost love between the Dutch and the Belgians either. He said our dog is a good, faithful watchdog that was protecting our family. Good dog he said. Said last time he was bitten by a dog was 71 years ago... in this same house!

He knows history. He came to sit with us.

These are not just ordinary days. Pray, sit with each other, adjust, be determined to bring folks to Christ's love and healing power... even if you have to take off the roof of the house.

Four sticks work. Some golf pros say a good way to practice is to play a round of golf with only a couple of sticks. You learn to use those sticks well. We don't have all the things that our large churches back home have to offer their people and communities. We have only a few sticks. But a few sticks are enough... may even help you to improve your game of Faith.

This is not just an ordinary week. Like the four, figure out a way to adjust and work together to help. May God give you the strength to sit with someone this week. And may God bring someone into your home to sit with you and provide solace for your spirit.

"You Don't Do WHAT?"

March 2, 2003

*It was a normal week and the church bells rang
as always, which was nice in Boerdonk.*

Time to confess to you. Weeks ago I mentioned that there are two things in our marriage that Pam does not do. She does not do breakfast, and she will not iron those terrible-to-iron green military fatigues. I have gotten more comments from this one line than you can imagine.

Carol Jackson, a girl from the deep South and a sweetheart of a woman, is retired in Mississippi with her husband Matt. (Actually he is retired and she is teaching school full time!) Carol wrote and said she never knew it was an option for a wife to not do breakfast. Pam and I have had one of Carol's wonderful breakfasts on a Saturday morning in Massachusetts... thank God Carol never knew it was an option in marriage to not do breakfast. Elizabeth Withrow, in her nineties and living with some other same-aged women in Texas, read the entire eSERMON to her group of ladies in a house in Mexia, Texas. They eat lunch together and listen to a devotion while they eat each day. Elizabeth said they all liked the part about Pam not doing breakfasts and not ironing my military fatigues. They liked

195

hearing of a man cooking waffles for 27 years. Said they enjoyed hearing of different ways things could be done. Some ladies wrote and simply told Pam "You go, girl!"

Another person, General Leslie Kenne, got right to the point.

"Gary, what do YOU not do?"

I have not been able to come up with the answer to her question. I wrote Gen. Kenne and told her I would get back to her... weeks ago. Told her I would mention it in a sermon... bought me some time to come up with an answer. Finally I asked Pam. Told her I wanted to mention her answer in a sermon and that I wanted to give her a week to come up with an answer. About a half second later she answered... the immediacy of the answer concerned me. Pam seemed eager to answer General Kenne's question.

Today is the last Sunday before Fat Tuesday. Last Sunday before Ash Wednesday. Last Sunday before the six weeks of Lent. Here in this part of the world these days are called Carnival. One huge party before Ash Wednesday and six weeks of fasting and prayer focus.

School is out for the week. Businesses will be closed. I even asked our grocery truck deliveryman Sanders if he was running the truck this week or shutting down. "Not driving this week. Carnival." And he smiled.

What is all this talk of fasting and praying? In this morning's Scripture reading, folks wanted to know why John's disciples and the Pharisees were "accustomed" to fasting and why the disciples of Jesus were not fasting so much.[1] The disciples of Jesus were eating, laughing, having a wonderful time, listening to stories... pretty relaxed group. A group that was not doing the customary religious thing of fasting, wearing a long face, and yelling of the impending ending of the world.

---

[1] Mark 2: 18-22

Some were fasting, and some were celebrating. Happened 2,000 years ago and still goes on. Some like Carnival, some don't. I like it. We never had anything like it in our farming communities in southern Ohio. I like the way Carnival, Ash Wednesday, Lent, and Easter all tie together. That is the way life is. Sort of all hangs together.

Jesus said His disciples would have their day when the Bridegroom would be gone and they would fast. On THAT day. Then He said that you have to put new wine into new wineskins. It's a time for a new idea and new wineskins to hold the new wine.

We always have questions and comments about the way we live our lives, don't we? Always curious about how others work out their faith, meld their differences in marriage, interpret their life of faith... we are a curious group aren't we? Jesus, what do YOUR Disciples NOT do? They seem to do everything. The questions linger on for all of us.

"You don't do what, Gary?" Pam's answer. Eagerly given. Three things.

One, you don't clean toilets. Two, you would not change dirty diapers... at least not for a long time after Amity was born." And three, you don't do needles."

Some things just are not fun to do. During 27 years of marriage I had never thought about what I don't do in marriage. It took an Air Force general to press the issue.

I don't do needles. Hate shots. The doctor told Pam she needed daily shots for a couple of weeks several years ago. Doctor said he would teach me how to give Pam the shots. Pam laughed... she had me drive her to her nurse friend's house... I sat in the car. A couple of years ago in Mississippi, kidney stones put me in the hospital. Sort of the male version of child birth. The attendants came into the room and I heard them say to the military medical trainee in the military hospital, "Here, I know you have never put in an IV before. We will train you and let you practice and learn on this guy." I moaned and squeezed Pam's hand. Pam stuck out her arm and said, "If you want to practice, use my arm."

God, how can one man be so lucky?

We are all different. We all work out our similarities and our differences in marriage, church, and life. Some fast. Some don't. Some celebrate, some don't.

Next Sunday you will be asked to come forward after the sermon and have a cross marked on your forehead with ashes. The ashes are from palm branches used in a Christian church to celebrate Palm Sunday and Easter. Some days you celebrate, some days you remember "ashes to ashes, dust to dust."

Some days you have around you those who give you strength, some days you don't.

Amity told us this past week she was with some people at Auburn as they talked about college life and stresses in such a life. She first commented she had not been under much stress last year... then she remembered. She is a strong girl, very strong girl... with a great sense of humor. She then added to her answer, "No stress. Well, there was one thing. My parents left me." And she laughed as she told that her Air Force parents moved over to Europe right after 9/11 happened.

We did leave her.

After 27 years of marriage, you know everything about each other. Wrong. Still learning. I came home one day this week, and Pam met me at the door and said she had some very sad news. I could tell by her face someone in the family had died. She told me Mr. Rogers had died. I then realized that to Pam, Mr. Rogers was family. She told me later that the last ten years of teaching she has been defending Mr. Rogers in the classroom... kids wanted more violence and less Mr. Rogers. I never knew she defended Mr. Rogers so. She said that eventually some kids would admit privately to her that Mr. Rogers was "cool" and that they watched him on TV... but would not admit it to their friends. Thank God for teachers like Pam.

I was so upset this week to hear that a teacher in Maine is telling her students whose military reservist parents have deployed that their parents are wrong, immoral, and unethical for going to war. She is supposedly telling them that in the classroom, and the kids are upset about it to the point where it has to be dealt with by the commanders of the parents who are deploying. I don't care how you feel about the war and politics - but telling young students such a thing in class while their parents have left them to serve in the military -- well, that is abusive.

Our world needs our prayers. John Ed Mathison, Senior Minister at Frazer United Methodist Church (UMC) in Montgomery, Alabama has both the Governor and the Lt. Governor of Alabama in his church. He leads a prayer group and Bible study in the State Capital building. The Governor and the Lt. Governor are from different political parties. John Ed says, "They are both godly people who need our prayers to lead the state."

Frazer UMC, with a huge ministry to military members at Maxwell and Gunter Air Force Base and also to the Air University students, has started a Military Family Care Group ministry under the leadership of Reverend Jim Salminen. Reverend Jim is a retired Air Force colonel who went to seminary and was ordained after a distinguished military career.

This is a church where John Ed told the story of a man in the church just diagnosed with cancer. The man's friend, in a halting attempt to comfort, said, "Man, cancer is big." The man, without hesitation, replied, "Yes, but God is bigger!"

That is what Lent is all about. To remember God is bigger than anything we face in life.

Yes, we did leave Amity. But we left her in bigger hands than our own. She is in God's hands and in the church's hands. God is bigger than our parents' leaving us. Amity told us she and her roommate have been going to church every Sunday this semester at the large Baptist church that has 500 Auburn students in it. She gets it.

Lent is a time to remember how wonderful it is to be a part of this thing called Church. Great to be a part of a Family where an Air Force general can say to a chaplain, "Well, what do you NOT do?" Great to be a part of a Family that can produce teachers that can tell students around the world that it is "cool" to watch a TV show where some nice guy wears the same sweater and sneakers every day and invites you to think of the world as a neighborhood.

As you know, Mr. Rogers was a Presbyterian minister. Television commentators are saying we had no idea what we were hearing all those years when some snickered at Mr. Rogers. He was a genius. He saw what many did not see... the world as it could be.

"What do YOU not do?" is a great question. Think about it. Next Sunday, after Carnival, you will be asked what you are giving up for Lent. One guy in one church gave up spinach for Lent. His wife declared publicly, "You HATE spinach." He grinned and said, "I know."

Whatever you face this week at work, at home, at school, or in the world... God is bigger. That is the Good News. Have a good week. I will be cleaning toilets this week. But don't bring me any dirty diapers. I am too old.

"Why Are The Dutch So Happy?"

May 4, 2003

I think it would be good if more American towns and cities had large church bells to help mark the pace of life and slow us all down a bit. That is what happens in Boerdonk... the church bells slow down life for these wonderful people.

He is Risen! He is Risen, Indeed! Easter continues in the church calendar and in our hearts and lives! He is Risen! He is Risen, Indeed!

This morning Peter is preaching and telling the folks in the book of Acts that they should repent.[1] He is telling them they crucified the wrong man. They put to death Jesus instead of the convicted murderer. He is telling them now how they should act as a group. Preaching is funny... telling folks how you should act as a group.

We Americans don't like to be told how to act or what to do. Freedom is what we value. And rightly so. To a

---

[1] Acts 3:13-19

point. Peter reminds us we are accountable. Freedom comes through accountability.

We have been having a discussion in our family over the last couple of weeks. Daniel asked me, "Why are the Dutch so happy, Dad? I am happy and positive, but why are the Dutch kids always so happy. All of them are happy here in Boerdonk. Why?"

Great question.

One reason they are happy is they have a cultural mayor whose job is to direct the village and make sure folks do what they are SUPPOSED to do. Last year our neighbor's newborn baby died. The mayor of Boerdonk, our landlord Toon, immediately came to OUR house and told us what to do for the neighbor. He told us when to visit, what to do, and he also let us know that if we did not visit as expected that HE would find out. We did as he told us.

Folks in Boerdonk are EXPECTED to act right and to treat each other properly. I don't know about you, but I like that. Accountability as individuals to a group is a good thing to me. Toon tells folks how to act. Peter was telling folks in the Book of Acts how to act.

Moses brought down Ten Commandments on stone tablets from the mountaintop and TOLD people to follow these laws... telling folks what they were supposed to do. Many of the Laws of Moses were relational... how the members of the group were to treat each other. And how to relate to God.

Why are the Dutch so happy? In Boerdonk, they value family above all else. I asked my landlord's son, Pedro, why he only works four days a week when he could do as we Americans do and work six or seven days a week and make much more money. He replied, "I only work four days a week so I can be with my kids the other three days." I asked

202

him if he has plenty of money. He said, "Enough." I asked him if he was going to have plenty of money for retirement. He said, "Enough." There was that "enough" word again.

Kids in Boerdonk are happy because they have lots of parental time. Secure they are. Parents walk their kids to the village school right across the street from our house each day. Kids laughing and playing while parents visit on the school grounds... kids know their parents will be there at 12 noon to pick them up for lunch. Kids know they are valued above all else. Happy kids. Contented kids.

Boerdonk families do not change houses or jobs. Our 24-year old grocery truck man Sanders just built a new house that he will never pay off in his lifetime. Different mortgage system over here. I asked him how long he would stay in that same house. "My whole life" was his answer. His dad lives in the same house he was born in, which is across the street from us. I asked Sanders how long he will remain in business with his dad and brother as grocer for three villages, delivering groceries six days a week. "My whole life. I cannot imagine being happier doing anything else. Life is no better than doing what I am doing in Boerdonk." And he grinned. I look forward to seeing him EVERY Saturday as he delivers groceries like clockwork. Like the church clock that chimes and rings every half-hour 24/7/365 forever. Happy folks these Boerdonk people are.

Our heater repairman is the same guy who installed the different heating systems in this house over the last 39 years. He responds within 30 minutes of being called. Always cheerful. He talked our landlord into letting him install hot water for our American washing machine, running the hot water line off the steam heater. He is in business with his father and brother. Happy heating-system men.

They go to church together as a village. The whole village. There is only one church for them... the village Catholic Church. Every village here in this part of Holland has one Catholic church because most are Catholic, one bike shop because everyone owns a bike, one café because everyone likes to eat, one cemetery because everyone ends up there.

Cleanliness is next to godliness and leads to happiness. The Dutch clean their windows religiously every week. Spotless windows are the pride of the Dutch. And they know when the Americans residents do NOT clean their windows religiously. They let us know when our windows could use some help, when our rose bushes could use some trimming, when the weeds need some attention in our flower garden. I love it. Funny at first, but now such "direction" is comforting. Yards and even dirt in the small yards are raked weekly. Small houses and lots, but each immaculate. Every yard in the village is a showpiece.

At the annual neighborhood dinner (which every neighborhood in Boerdonk organizes), I commented to one pretty young blonde Dutch woman about the "weekly hobby of cleaning windows." She replied with a snap, "I don't do windows weekly and it is NOT a hobby to me." Times are changing even for the Dutch!

My mother demanded I keep my room clean, my clothes picked up, closets organized... I even had to make my bed every morning before going to school. Most everything good that has been accomplished in my life can be traced back to what my mother demanded of me. She raised us four boys on her own to be organized, responsible, and clean. Basic military training for me was a cake walk... my mom could have trained the instructors. She is a fanatically clean person... and that is a compliment. I told her if she ever visited Holland she would be in heaven... that she would be with 17 million Dutch citizens who were just like her... cleanliness is godliness!

Table napkins were invented by the Dutch. Cleanliness.

Look up the word "frugal" in the dictionary, and you see a picture of a Dutch couple. Law limits how much trash a person here can have. One trash can per two weeks is the limit... any more than that gets left on your front door by the trash man. We know from experience. Took us a few weeks to cut down and quit accumulating so much stuff and trash. Recycling is part of our life now.

Everyone tells us how to live. We are accountable to the group. Kids are happy. They know their place in the group. Security comes from knowing your place in the group. Families in Boerdonk eat dinner at 5:00 pm... all at the same time... so the kids can play together at the same time before and after dinner. Happiness is predictability and security. The Dutch have two Christmases and two Easters. Christmas #1 on December 25th is for immediate family to gather and eat and celebrate. Christmas #2 on December 26th is for extended family to gather and eat and celebrate. Same with Easter #1 and #2, Sunday and Monday, with Monday Easter #2 being a national holiday.

Pam and I just celebrated Easter #1. Great celebration. Fifteen-hour day, five hours of driving to three countries, two worship services and three sermons, two potluck dinners. We were exhausted after Easter #1 and wanted to get more stuff done on Easter #2... we were Americans with a schedule. Things to do to get ready for our July move to Texas. On the go.

Our landlord and his family were sitting outside in the sun as extended family on Easter #2 when Pam and I arrived home from work. They were wasting the day away, laughing, drinking special Easter beverage (whipped egg yolk with cream), visiting, and enjoying the sun. They invited us over... we declined. They insisted we join them. They were gathered around Toon our landlord who is fighting cancer. He looked happier than we had seen him in a while. Family all gathered around him.

We joined them. Cried with them and Toon a bit. Laughed with them a lot. Showed them photos of our families (which they asked to see again) in Ohio and Texas.

We wasted five hours of our day with them. You know it was not a waste. You know that is the best way to spend a day. They know. That is why Boerdonk folks are so happy, Daniel. They know how to spend their money frugally and their time wastefully. Wisely. With family. Laughing. Crying. The kids were happy. The bells rang.

The Europeans know the truth in fairy tales. They still read Little Red Riding Hood to their kids to teach their kids that there are wolves out there in the world that dress up like innocent-looking grandmothers... and that the wolves are dangerous and will devour you if you are not careful. They hate war and don't want this war, but at the same time they are glad Saddam is being taken care of. They remember World War I, where they were able to stay neutral. They remember World War II when their country was run over by a maniac who stole their freedom, their bikes, their lands, and their musical instruments... all cherished parts of their soul as a nation. They know there are wolves out there.

They know it takes an America and its military to protect them and their wonderfully docile, passive type of country. They are strong and smart people. Sander asked if I was going to Iraq. I told him the Volkel American soldiers were staying in place in Holland. He said, "Ah, so you can take care and protect we Dutch, huh?" I told him it was so the Dutch could also take care of us. He laughed and then told us how glad he and the others are that we Americans were here in Holland.

It takes an America to rid the world of wolves in order for places like Holland to survive and exist. We all understand that.

Humor is rampant with the Dutch in Boerdonk. Toon's family told us of the upcoming holiday called "Queen's Day" celebrating the Queen's birthday. They wanted to know if we Americans celebrated "President Bush Day." They laughed at their own question.

A natural gas find in northern Netherlands equivalent to Saudi oil underwrites some of the socialized medicine and economy they have here. A flat 19% tax on everything brings in more revenue for the government. Huge taxes on all personal income over $50,000 generate more revenue. Seems to work well here in addition to having the American military presence to supplement their own small military.

Any country that has Christmas #1 and Christmas #2 and Easter #1 and Easter #2 can't be too bad... so, Daniel, these may be some of the reasons why the Dutch are so happy.

And they got their musical instruments back after World War II. And they are still celebrating. When folks sing, play musical instruments, and sit around wasting time with family and friends... well, that leads to happiness.

And they got their bikes back after WW II. They ride still with a smile on their faces. Life is good if you have family, a church, a musical instrument, and a bike.

And with a guy like Toon and the Apostle Peter around reminding us of how we should so order and live our lives, then we have much to celebrate! Let's sing. And then go home and maybe clean our windows... or maybe not! Amen.

Letter 32

Looking for the Chicken with 100 Legs

May 25, 2003

Polish villages also have incredibly beautiful churches and the joyous and constant church bells, as we found out.

Jesus told us what we are supposed to do as Christians and then He said that if we do those things the world would be changed. Folks will recover, we will not walk around fearfully, folks will be affected by our actions and deeds, healing will take place. Fanciful thinking this sounds like to some.

Jesus was crucified and died. Then He rose again and was alive. Now today on Ascension Sunday we read in the book of Acts that He left the Disciples again on this earth alone as He Ascended into Heaven... every Sunday we recite the Apostle's Creed and one line says, "He ascended into Heaven and is seated at the right hand of the Father... he will come again to judge the living and the dead."

Alive, dead, alive again after the Resurrection... and now leaving just when the Disciples thought He was here to stay. You can see the Ascension Stone in Jerusalem from which Jesus is said to have ascended into Heaven. The

209

Disciples did not want Him to leave them again. Their life with Him was a yo-yo cycle of His being there, not there, there, now leaving again.

Today is Ascension Sunday... we celebrate that He went to be with the Father and that He will come again to judge the Living and the Dead.

And the gospel writer, Mark, says that right before Jesus ascended into Heaven, he gave them a "final" pep talk... a farewell speech.[1] He told them to go baptize, to be bold, tell the whole world and proclaim the gospel to every creature... and that these signs would follow them and us. That we would drive out demons, speak new languages, have no fear so much that even serpents will not hold us captive, drink will not own us, and that we will overcome sickness."

Quite a game speech. Go get 'em, Church. Speak new languages? Heal folks? Have no fear? Go into the whole world? Man, this guy Jesus was dreaming. He was caught up in the moment. A bit excited and overstated.

I did not want to be in Air Command and Staff College (ACSC) in 1993 studying war for an entire year. My Montgomery neighbor asked me one morning when he saw the cross on my Air Force uniform, "What is a chaplain doing studying war?" I told him I had no idea what I was doing in a War College. I wanted to be in the chapel doing what a pastor/chaplain is supposed to be doing... studying peace and doing God's work.

There were 250 officers in ACSC from around the world. Cream of the crop types, all except us four chaplains. We were out of place and only there by accident. I wanted to go back to the church where it is safe and war-free.

---

[1] Mark 16:15-20

Jacek sat by me in our seminar of 13 officers from around the country and world for the entire year. Jacek was an officer from the formerly communist-controlled country of Poland. Fighter pilot. An officer chiseled out of stone... perfect military officer. Professional soccer player. Ran 10 miles a day to keep in shape. A gentle man. A genius. He had only learned the English language three months earlier prior to ACSC and was leading our seminar in studies and tests and papers, carrying students like me academically.

He loved Pam's cooking and we enjoyed having him in our home for dinners and events. He spoke of his wife Marzena and daughters Irmina, Kinza, and Kornelia, who were not allowed to accompany him to America for the 15 months he was there to attend two consecutive military schools. He spoke of his family's apple orchard in eastern Poland and of how he missed it all. He used his one trip home one month before gradation from ACSC... to attend Irmina's Confirmation ceremony in the Catholic Church. Did not want to miss it.

Jesus was dreaming. Speak new languages, heal people, and be free from fear? Right, Jesus. Jesus told us to do what WE are supposed to do as a church and He will do the rest.

Never dreamed in '93 that in the year 2003 Pam, Amity, and I would be sitting in Jacek's house in Poland with his wife Marzena and their daughters... eating dinner. (Daniel stayed back in Holland with friends... too much traveling for him, he said!) Two weeks ago our visit to Poland and to Jacek's house was one of the most remarkable and meaningful trips Pam and I have ever taken. We ate an apple from his orchard served to us by Jacek's father and mother. Saw the church where Pope John Paul II was priest and the town and school where he was educated and raised. Saw the cathedral in Krakow where the Pope was Cardinal. Saw the new house Jacek and his father built which includes a prayer garden in the yard with a statue of Mary for a place of prayer and focus and meditation. His dad finished the house in 1993 while Jacek was over in America trying to help me make it through ACSC studying war and peace.

We stood 400 feet beneath the surface of the earth in a 1,000-year old salt mine where over 270 million tons of salt have been mined... where the church carved chapels and incredibly beautiful Biblical figures out of the salt caverns so the miners could worship and have Mass 400 feet beneath the ground as they worked day and night.

The church was doing what it was supposed to do where the people were... underground working.

The church was there. Underground. The tour guide let me go where no one is supposed to go and have my picture taken... he pulled up the boundary rope and motioned for me to go stand in the salt pulpit which is off-limits to the public... after Jacek told him in Polish that I was a "priest/minister of the church." Rules were adjusted for my camera and me! I stood there in the underground chapel pulpit... a pulpit made of salt. Solid salt.

Jesus said we are the salt of the earth. Chapels carved of salt. Jesus would have loved the symbolism.

It has been a long 60+ years for the Church in Poland. It had to function underground but yet it grew stronger and stronger during this time. Jacek introduced us to a priest who said his churches are packed with people these days. Jacek showed us the Jewish mass cemetery near his house... with the Tree of Life in the stonework surrounding this place. The message could not be killed... the Tree of Life speaks to that, quietly and solidly.

Jacek's wife Marzena cooked and served multi-course meals to us. Our last evening there we sat down for dinner and eventually got to the main course. First we went through soup, pickled garlic, vegetables, various wines, and breads... and then came the pork, sausage, and chicken breasts.

Jacek passed the chicken breasts to us and commented about days under the communist regime when the government's food distribution system was a bit lacking and the butt of jokes. Food was supposed to be distributed evenly to every citizen -- that was the theory. But it did not quite work that way. All that ever made it to the common people's table and level were the chicken legs... no chicken breasts were available to the people. Only legs. Someone high in the distribution system got the chicken breasts and the common people got hundreds of legs.

Jacek said the joke of the people was that they would love to see the chicken with 100 legs someday. They had never seen chicken breasts on their table, only hundreds of legs over the years.

To have chicken breasts on the table for us was a sign of the changing times in Poland. Jacek took us to McDonald's one time... said with a grin, "McDonald's is the first sign of democracy having arrived in a country." And I had a chicken breast sandwich.

The Church never gave up during these last 60 years in Poland.

Jacek showed me the commemorative cross marking the date in 1939 when the invading enemies executed 20,000 Polish military officers. 20,000.

The church never gave up. It kept doing what it was supposed to do. It has done it for 2,000 years since the Ascension of Christ. Building chapels underground. Operating underground. Jacek's grandfather remained imprisoned after WWII because be had resisted the invaders and had operated underground. Jacek's aunt just gave Jacek his grandfather's diary journaling his recording of events and thoughts of those days. Jacek asked me to someday consider helping him write his grandfather's and his own story.

I had lots of fun with Jacek in ACSC with saying, "Is this (America) a great country or what?" and we would all laugh together as we watched him enjoy America.

Last week we so enjoyed realizing our dream of seeing his country and having chicken breasts and apples with him and his family. He took us to a town where local people create beautiful icons and pieces of church art.

The church never stopped doing what it was supposed to do there in Poland... now they can do it openly and with freedom which is so embraced and cherished now.

May God give us the strength on this Ascension Sunday and this week to do what we are supposed to do as a church. Heal, have no fear, speak a new language of love and Hope, and help folks recover... Jesus said we could do it. And do it boldly and with no fear.

Have an apple today and a piece of chicken breast sometime this week. God is doing all kinds of miracles around us as He promised... from St. Louis to San Marcos to Poland as people recover and are surrounded freely by the Church.

Toon, our landlord, is eating again, kissing Pam again, laughing again, and appreciates your prayers. He says your prayers combined with the radiation treatments for his cancer are working as he regains his zest for life. He loves it when I tell him how many of you around the world pray for him.

Let's keep doing what we are supposed to be doing as a church. Pray and care.

The Next Chapter of Life

July 2003 - Present

In December of 2002, we received an email in Boerdonk in response to our Christmas letter. A minister in San Marcos, Texas, emailed and told us he had resigned from his church. Pam and I talked again, as we had for some time now, about how someday we would be making the move from this nomadic military lifestyle to a (hopefully) more stable and permanent life of pastoring a church in a city somewhere.

We had talked of how we would like to be able to "settle down" and keep Daniel in one school for his entire high school career. He had been to four schools in three years and three schools in two years following 9/11, and it did not promise to get any better for military families in the near future.

So we were hoping to settle down in a civilian church somewhere for a while. Hopefully for a long, long time.

I submitted my resume to the church relocation system in regards to the San Marcos church in January 2003. I stated on my resume that one of my goals in life was to "plant a tree and watch it grow," meaning I was hoping to stay in one place for a long, long time. Soon the resume went national and I surprisingly got calls from Kentucky and other states. I declined them all, just wanting to pursue the San Marcos position. There were 43 candidates for that position, so I did not expect to be "in the running." In March of 2003, on the day the war in Iraq was starting, Pam and I boarded a plane to fly to San Marcos and meet with church leaders there.

We found it very safe to fly that day. Very few others were flying, so we had wonderful and personalized service from all flight attendants. Security was excellent because of the world situation, and because there were NO lines at any international airports, we went quickly through all check points and metal detectors that day! The church search committee was surprised we showed up in light of the beginning of the war, but we told them while it was odd to fly at such a time, it turned out to be a rather quiet and secure flight.

Our son Daniel was on an 8-day school ski trip to Austria. We asked him if he would be scared if we traveled to the United States for a week while he was skiing in Austria on his Eindhoven International School junior high ski trip. He said, "Mom and Dad, I will be skiing in the Alps... I don't care WHERE in the world you are! Go and have fun!"

We departed Boerdonk on Tuesday and arrived in San Marcos on Wednesday, interviewed Thursday with the church Search Committee, met with three members of the Salary Negotiation team on Friday, and they made their verbal and written promises. We met with the Board on Saturday, I preached Sunday at both services, looked at eight houses Sunday afternoon and evening, selected a house just under construction on Monday, signed purchase papers on house Monday afternoon, got financing approved Tuesday morning, and returned back to Boerdonk Wednesday.

The Search Committee voted unanimously to offer us the position, the salary negotiation members seemed trustworthy and the negotiations were smooth and efficient, the Board voted unanimously 16-0 to "call us" to come be their minister family, and two weeks later the congregation voted 172-1 to extend to us a "call" to come. The lone vote against "calling" me was from a church member who supported the war and felt the church should not be calling a chaplain away from the military at a time of war.

That had been an issue with us also. I was torn between continuing to serve the men, women, and children of military families and the option of returning to civilian ministry. Any good chaplain, in my opinion, is torn by the issue. I had served 31 years in the Air Force (7 as an enlisted person, 5 as a reservist, and 19 years as a chaplain). I loved serving the people of the uniform as a chaplain.

Ministers are on "loan" from the church to the military and always remain legally under the jurisdiction of the church. We chaplains are paid by the military but "owned" by the church because of separation of church and state issues. The singular reason a minister is "loaned" to the military is to provide religious freedom expression opportunities (guaranteed to all U.S. citizens under First Amendment Freedom of Religion decision) to the men and women in uniform while they are serving our country on active duty and away from their home church. Chaplains cannot, by law, be used for any other purpose in the military except to provide religious services to men and women in uniform. We cannot command troops (at least in the Air Force) and we cannot carry firearms or any weaponry.

Some have asked, "How could one be a person of the (ministerial) cloth and a person of peace and also serve in the military war machine?" Good question. My answer is a simple short story that best illustrates the issue.

One Lutheran chaplain friend tells of the day he was serving a Lutheran church and was an active anti-military protestor during Viet Nam. He purposely went on a tour of a nuclear missile silo out west... just to heckle the "war mongers," the young officers with their fingers on the nuclear buttons down in the silo.

The Lutheran anti-war activist asked a young officer during the tour, "How can you come to work each day wanting to go to war and knowing you could push that button and destroy millions?"

The officer immediately replied, "Sir, I come to work each day PRAYING for peace and PRAYING I don't have to push the war button."

That Lutheran minister is now an excellent Air Force chaplain who served with distinction in Desert Storm. A fighter pilot ACSC classmate who served in Desert Storm told me of that chaplain and said the chaplain always stood in the same spot at 2 a.m. each morning as flight crews went out to their planes for early morning missions. Same pilot told me he and the other pilots put their own lives on the line and took a more dangerous flight pattern to avoid flying over housing areas where civilians lived... they instead took the most dangerous route over enemy fire toward their targets rather than endangering enemy families. You don't want a military without a chaplaincy there as a conscience.

One morning the flight crews had to scramble early and the chaplain had not yet been notified. When he heard the sirens go off, he grabbed a truck at 0130 hours (1:30 a.m.) and raced to the flight line. The pilots were purposely delaying their take-off... they felt better with the nightly send-off ritual of the chaplain. They had run by "the chaplain's spot on the flightline, and he was not there."

War pilots are men and women of ritual. Whatever gets them home safely from one mission they want to do each mission. Use the same shampoo. Put socks on in the same order. Be blessed by the chaplain in his spot each morning on the way to the plane.

The chaplain climbed the ladder of every fighter jet in the dark and shook the hands of each pilot and prayed with each one... for world peace and for safety for all. Think about that image.

My 31-years-of-military-service opinion and ministerial opinion is that by far most U.S. military officers come to work praying literally FOR peace and seek to pass on a peaceful world to their own children.

The Dutch are such a peaceful people. They love peace and are a peaceful and tranquil people. I read one statistic that said the Dutch people are the most contented nation of people found by folks who research that kind of thing. I believe it. Yet the Dutch remember vividly times when their country was overrun by wolves at least twice in the past one hundred years. They, by and large, pray for peace, support the American military presence, and remember and hope for continued tranquility in their little villages.

Four months after my March interview we moved to San Marcos (July 2003) and into our newly finished house.

As we pulled out of Boerdonk for the last time in July, I could hardly look at the church or listen to the bells for the last time. I had fallen in love with both. I could hardly look at Toon as he hugged Pam and me and Daniel good-by. He had huge tears in his eyes. Such a kind and gentle man. I knew there would always be an emptiness in part of my heart from that day forward for me. There is. Thank God for the wonderful pictures we have of Toon and the church. The church bells ring in our hearts and minds to this day.

Just 18 months later, in March of 2005, I resigned from the "dream church" as pastor. I had done all I could do there. After I resigned, my wife asked, "What are we going to do?" I said, "I don't know what I am going to do, but I know what I am NOT going to do. We are not going to move our son to another school and we are not going to move out of this house."

Sometimes you may not know what you are going to do in life, but it can help to decide what you are not going to do at that point.

I wished for the solace and contemplative sounds of the Boerdonk church bells to remind me that we were not alone in life.

On March 10, two days after I resigned, we flew to Hawaii to officiate and attend Amity's wedding to Frank Crnko. What a wonderful ceremony there on the beach!

The next month, in April of 2005, Christ the Redeemer Church formed in San Marcos, with 20 families and 85 charter members, and they asked if I would be their minister. Pam and Daniel and I were honored to be asked to be their ministerial family.

I have not yet planted my tree here in San Marcos, but plan to do so in the fall of 2006.

In San Marcos, we listen to train whistles at night, but we yearn for the solace of the church bells. We are slowly growing accustomed to the train whistles. When a train goes by blowing its whistle less than a block away from our church service on Sundays and the people cannot hear the sermon, I lovingly refer to the train whistle as "our church bells."

Epilogue

Toon (pronounced "tone")

Our Boerdonk landlord, Toon, passed away from lung cancer at age 78 after we returned to the United States. I can not bear the thought of a Boerdonk without Toon's smile, love of life, and presence. He ran the village café that his father and grandfather and great-grandfather had owned. The first thing he showed me when I entered his café for the first time was a Certificate on the wall... signed by the Pope, thanking Toon for his support on some Vatican matter. Toon loved the Church, insisted Pam and I attend his 50th wedding anniversary celebration at the Catholic Mass where he seated us as special guests, and he loved peace. He served as a military man for a brief period during World War II, but did not last long and was sent home. Though he never told me, I suspect or imagine that he was such a gentle person that the military world of World War II just broke his heart. I may be wrong. But he so loved people, so loved life, so believed in the Goodness of God and the Lord that I imagine war was hell for him. As I mentioned in a letter earlier about him, Toon told me he remembers standing in the streets of Boerdonk during the war and watching U.S. soldiers hanging in the air in their parachutes, being shot out of the sky by the enemy. Tears would fill his eyes as he told me this story. He said he and his father prayed that enough American soldiers would survive the jumps that they could free the Dutch people.

He loved to hug Pam. And he loved to dance with her and all the women. He hosted a dance every Saturday night in his café and had done so for over 55 years. Every Saturday night. We would go to bed at 11 p.m., and he and his café full of dancing villagers would just be getting started. They are still celebrating WWII being over and over getting their musical instruments and bicycles back. They would dance and eat until 4 a.m. and then be at Mass at 10:00 a.m. Same routine each Saturday night. Wore Pam and me out!

I hated moving from Boerdonk, but our leaving allowed Toon to move himself and his wife Anne into the large beautiful house that we rented from them. Toon would never have asked us to move out... he was a man of his word. But his health was rapidly deteriorating and he mentioned to me once that he would love to move his wife from the little apartment in the café into our large house someday after we moved back to the United States. Had we stayed in Holland for three or four years, Toon would have died without getting to move his wife into a nice home prior to his death.

For Toon's funeral Mass, several U.S.A.F. military men and women attended to pay tribute to Toon. Lt. Col Derek Avance, U.S. commander at Volkel Air Base, reported to me that the church in Boerdonk was standing room only.

A poignant moment of the Mass was the pealing of the Boerdonk church bells in honor of Toon's life that was so precious to so many. I wish so badly to have been there to pay tribute to Toon. I was honored to know our American soldiers and friends proudly represented our country in that funeral celebration.

With Toon's arrival, Heaven has gained a saint and Boerdonk lost a real man of Faith. But his family still gathers each Sunday at the café and laughs and tells stories and admires the children playing and spends hours visiting. Just visiting. I miss those scenes of that family gathered and laughing and visiting.

(Below is a note from Toon's daughter-in-law Marja in Boerdonk)

222

Dear Gary and Pam,

Like you said in the book, I did cry of course, especially when it comes to Landlord Toon (he liked that title you gave to him and he told it often to people). You felt really what he was like. He had a big enough heart for a lot of people especially those who would respect him and the way he lived in Boerdonk for it was HIS Boerdonk where in the middle of the heart of it he was standing proud his almost whole life... it was his history and his whole future because that is where he wanted to die. Later on when he saw that he really was going to die, it was good that they moved into your house (after you moved back to the United States). We then shared a lot of precious time together, knowing that we had to share those moments because they would not last forever. He died with all of us around him (my young son Pim held him tight and cried because we told him many months from now the death would be real, but some thought it isn't good for such a small child to be told this, but I knew at that moment)...this is good holding each other when you have fun together and holding each other when it is time to say goodbye.

In the name of the whole family I say THANK YOU to pronounce and honor Toon in your book about our lives here in Boerdonk. TOON WOULD BE SO PROUD THAT I THINK IF THE BOOK WOULD BE TRANSLATED IN DUTCH HE WOULD SELL A LOT OF BOOKS!

Marja Tillaart

Jacek

In 2005, Jacek was selected as a general in the Polish Air Force. Not long after making general, he took a friend on a private plane ride, having promised for quite a while to take the friend on the joy ride. Jacek's wife and daughter were on the ground, watching Jacek pilot the plane. Shortly after take-off and in front of his wife and young daughter, something terrible went wrong with the plane, and Jacek and his passenger were both killed as the plane plummeted to the ground near Jacek's family.

I still cannot bear to type those words.

One of the highlights of my life and 31 years in the Air Force was meeting and becoming friends with Jacek, the Polish MIG pilot, and seeing him become responsible for overseeing the integration of Poland into NATO. Father, lover of peace who was deeply hopeful that his own daughters would grow up with the freedom to worship the Lord he so loved openly and without fear. It was a dream come true for us to actually eat dinner in his new house (built in 1993) in 2003, eating apples from his own apple orchard in eastern Poland, praying in his Prayer Garden built in his FRONT yard (how many Americans have a prayer garden in their front yard?) of which he was so openly proud to have built, and listening to his stories of how oppressed the country was between WW II and 1989 when the Cold War ended. He was brilliant enough to be able to use humor to cope with the oppression and to still use humor to pass on the stories of those days he so celebrated as being over.

While we were classmates at ACSC for that year, Jacek asked me a considerable number of questions about the military chaplaincy structure in our country. Poland did not have such a thing due to communist party policies. He was most curious how this arrangement was structured and how it actually worked. He told me he was interested in bringing such a thing as a chaplaincy to the Polish military structure.

Jacek had revealed to me and the class in 1993 that he was not going to go home for Christmas on our two-week break from classes. He was, instead, going to go home in May for his daughter's confirmation in the Catholic Church. He said, "I will not miss that moment." That was when he revealed to us quietly for the first time that he was a Christian.

Since Jacek had such a grand sense of humor and was so curious about the chaplaincy and matters of faith, I played a word trick on him once I found out he was not going home for Christmas.

I asked him, "Jacek, how would you like to go to Purgatory with an American military chaplain?" He frowned and replied, "Ah, I would rather go to Paradise." I smiled and said, "Go with me to Purgatory and you will forget all this talk of Paradise."

He went with our family over Christmas to Purgatory. I explained to him that Purgatory was a favorite ski resort in Colorado. He got permission through his embassy officials to travel with us to Purgatory Ski Resort. We went through San Antonio, Texas on the way to rendezvous with Pam's parents and Tom and Dawn Bush, two retired Air Force chaplain families. San Antonio was lit up with marvelous Christmas lights on the River Walk. Jacek saw that beauty and said, "Ah, why can't ACSC be in San Antonio?"

He enjoyed Purgatory but made it clear he still wanted to go to Paradise someday. On Christmas Eve at Purgatory, we three minister families "broke bread and had communion" there in our ski condominium room around the fireplace. I was not sure Jacek would feel comfortable participating. We had not talked deeply about such faith matters. He did take communion that Christmas Eve. We prayed for World Peace. Picture that. Who would have imagined such a thing just a few years ago?

I rode with him on a boat in the ocean near Keesler Air Force Base in 2002. Linzy and Brenda Laughhunn, another chaplain family, owned a boat that provided lots of fun times for us chaplain families. Jacek had never been in or driven a boat in Poland. I still remember vividly fighter pilot Jacek delicately driving that boat in large waves. He was smiling with a huge grin, making that boat dance with the waves so gently. He rode the waves gently with the deftness of a fighter pilot making a fighter jet dance in and glide through the clouds.

Jacek had such high hopes for his nation. When we visited him in Poland, he was so proud to show us all the churches. The Catholic Church in Poland is not able to build enough churches right now to hold the worshipping community of Faith. Jacek showed me the cemetery where many Jewish are buried. His grandfather was a strong man of Christian faith during that time when it was not acceptable to be publicly expressive of one's faith. He showed us the church where Pope John grew up. Jacek's family helped the Jewish families in Poland during WWII.

He had such high hopes for his daughters, all three of them. He brought them to Montgomery, Alabama, in 1999 for one year Air War College. Had no house and no furniture. Poland let him bring his family this time (family was not allowed to come with him in 1993 for that one year military school) but money was scarce, and he was concerned about what kind of house he would be able to afford and where he could borrow some furniture. Jacek was so excited about being able to send his daughters to an American school for one year and for them to learn English.

Jacek rented a house we still owned in Montgomery. Jacek was concerned about furniture, about not having any. I called Tom Bartels immediately. Tom and his wife Karen live next door to our rental house and they are strong people of faith who attend Frazer United Methodist Church. The entire 8,000 member church is a community that practices helping others without reservation. I asked Tom if his Frazer Sunday School class could loan any furniture to Jacek and his family. Tom said, "We will make it happen." Tom is like that... son of a Lutheran pastor in Indiana, where his Lutheran father pastored a church and was the principal of the Lutheran school that educated and shaped Tom into the man of faith and action he is today.

Within a few days, Tom called me back and said every member of the Sunday School class at Frazer had volunteered to furnish a room for the Jacek house. Boy, did they furnish it! China, crystal, color TV's, couches, dining room furniture made IN Poland (Jacek was so thrilled he showed me the "Made in Poland" stamp on the underside of the chairs!), linens, beds, computer, etc. Tom and Karen's class moved the furniture into the house, complete with feminine furniture for the three girls, set the entire house up, and the completely furnished house was waiting for Jacek and his family when they arrived in Montgomery from Poland. Including very nice silverware. Jacek was overwhelmed by such generosity from the Church family.

Jacek was overwhelmed and always commented to me on that act of American and Christian generosity that the Frazer United Methodist Church Sunday School class displayed.

Jacek told me in 1999 that one of the highlights of his life was sharing the Holy Act of the Communion that night in Purgatory with three United States military chaplain families and being served bread and wine by three U.S. Air Force chaplains. It is one of the most poignant and significant memories of my life also.

Jacek is in the Paradise he so desired to see someday. One friend commented, after reviewing this section about Jacek's life, "Well, he continues to live on through this story and continues to watch over his three daughters and his wife." So he does. I hope Jacek knows this moment how deeply he affected my life.

The first time Amity had to go for dental work in Auburn after we moved to Holland, she told us she was a bit scared since she was used to having either her mother or me with her in the dental clinic. Since we were an ocean away, she carried an envelope with her into the dentist's chair and held on to the envelope while the drilling and dental work took place. The envelope was a letter from us... with our handwriting on it. She said holding the letter with our handwriting made her feel closer to us. The next visit she did not need to carry the envelope with her... she said she only needed the envelope for the first visit.

I hope that Toon's family and Jacek's family are able to hold onto the words in this book and feel some level of comfort for at least a brief moment.

I believe in angels. I believe Jacek and Toon are watching closely over their respective families. I am glad Toon departed this earth doing what he loved and being where he loved... with family on the hallowed ground called Boerdonk. I am glad Jacek departed this earth (if he had to) in the land of Poland he so loved, doing what he loved which was flying a plane in the sacred skies he so embraced and danced with many times, and being near the wife and daughters he so loved in Poland. I thank God Toon and Jacek were both doing what they loved to do in life to the end.

I can only imagine the moment when the Dutch man of Faith Toon and the Polish man of Faith Jacek met in the Kingdom on that Other Side in 2005. They both loved to hug, both loved to smile, both loved their families, both loved to speak quietly of their faith and the struggles of their respective countries, both loved the Church. They both loved.

Won't Heaven be wonderful filled with such people? I can hear the bells ringing up there, can't you?

When the Dutch are about to depart each other's company, they tilt their heads toward each other and simply say, "Success."

To each of you, in the love of God, I say, "Success."

About the Artist

Larry Weston

Over the years, Larry Weston has become recognized as one of the nation's leading artists. Many galleries and private collectors, here and abroad, seek his oil paintings and watercolors. His peers consider him a master of both the oil and watercolor painting techniques. He is an avid painter of what he considers "the hidden, quiet corners of the world". Through the selection of his subjects, the use of dramatic lighting and the subtle use of colors, many of his works have quiet, restful, and serene qualities. America's landscapes and the modern day cowboy are among his favorite subjects. He has also traveled and painted extensively throughout Europe and Mexico and the influence of these cultures can often be found in his work.

This outstanding artist is also well known for his teaching skills. For a number of years Larry was a traveling instructor for the University of Oklahoma's Continuing Education Department conducting painting workshops both here and abroad. In all, Larry has conducted over

500 oil and watercolor painting workshops. Much of his work has been seen in national art publications, feature newspaper articles and is currently represented in three of North Light Book art publications. Larry taped over 50 weekly TV programs titled "Adventures in Watercolor". This series was extremely popular among art students and the viewing public and was broadcast for three-years by popular demand as reruns in the Dallas/Fort Worth area, mid-west and eastern coast of the United States. Larry has served as judge in many local, regional, and national art shows.

Larry was born and raised in Phoenix, Arizona. His parents recognized his talents at an early age and enrolled him in oil painting classes when he was in the first grade. Larry has been painting ever since. He and his wife, Shirley, recently moved from the Dallas area and now reside in San Marcos, Texas. He is a signature member and a past President of the Southwestern Watercolor Society and a member of many other well-known national art organizations.

How Larry Weston met Boerdonk... and brought it to Life!

The manuscript for this <u>Letters from Boerdonk</u> was mostly finished (letters compiled and arranged in order) by fall of 2005. But HighPoint Publishing Company staff and I agreed... it would take a special and talented artist to bring into being the sort of book cover and chapter illustrations that we envisioned for this book. We were stymied for several months over trying to find the right artist.

In December of 2005 during the week of Christmas, a new neighbor moved in directly across the street from us in San Marcos. Because of Christmas busyness and because of being gone on a church ski trip to Colorado, Pam and I did not get a chance to meet the new neighbors until the second week in January. I met Larry Weston while we were both taking out our respective trash cans to the street in that second week of January. Larry found out from that conversation that he had moved across the street from a minister. I found out I now had a new neighbor that was an artist. We found out we had both been in the Air Force and we spent some time discussing airplanes and our affinity for Europe.

Pam and I soon were taking Larry and his wife Shirley out for dinner each week to introduce them to good restaurants in the area. It was a lot of fun to meet someone new and nice and to have the pleasure of some good company. As the relationship grew, so did we four... literally.

Then I saw Larry's paintings in his house. His house was a gallery of incredibly beautiful and stunning paintings... all done by him! I called Milena and Ken at HighPoint and said, "I think God may have brought somebody into our lives that you will want to meet."

<u>Letters from Boerdonk</u> changed dramatically for the better that day in February of 2006. Larry had moved to "quiet" San Marcos from the Dallas area to paint be closer to

the galleries around central Texas that carried his paintings, and to slow down a bit in life. After he read the "Boerdonk" manuscript and, much to the delight of HighPoint staff and me, he agreed to create drawings to introduce each chapter within the book and was also commissioned to do two oil paintings for the front and back book covers. Early in 1982 Larry resigned from Otis Engineering a Halliburton company as the Graphic Arts Manager, in order to pursue a full time career as a fine arts artist and art instructor in oil and watercolor painting. Dusting off his graphic arts skills he poured himself into this book and the results are nothing less than spectacular.

When I showed Duane DeWald the manuscript for the "Boerdonk" book and asked him, as a life-long friend, if he was interested in coming aboard on the book project as a marketing expert, he seemed somewhat interested. When I showed him some illustrations that Larry had drawn for the "Boerdonk" book, then Duane got VERY interested and enthused. Larry's art brought Duane in on the project. When Nelwyn Moore was handed the manuscript of "Boerdonk" to proof, I purposely showed her the then separate drawings (not yet integrated into manuscript) that Larry had done. Without even reading any of the manuscript, she commented immediately that she would buy the book simply for Larry's artwork! At that point, neither Duane nor Nelwyn knew about Larry's art background!

We are all deeply grateful to the One who brought our paths together with Larry and Shirley Weston.

Gary Smith

July 26, 2006

About the Author

Gary Layne Smith

Gary Layne Smith, a native of Dayton Ohio, graduated from nearby Bellbrook High School in 1971 and subsequently joined the U.S. Air Force as an enlisted airman. He received a Bachelor of Applied Arts and Science from Southwest Texas State University (now Texas State University) in San Marcos, Texas in 1980. He obtained a Master of Divinity graduate degree in 1984 from Brite Divinity School, with an emphasis on Pastoral Counseling.

Gary served as the Youth Minister at University United Methodist Church in Ft. Worth, Texas from 1981 to 1984 while attending seminary. He was ordained as a minister in 1984 in the Disciples of Christ Church in San Marcos, Texas (where he was previously Director of Youth Ministries while in undergraduate school). Gary then served as Minister of Evangelism at William C. Martin United Methodist Church in Bedford, Texas in 1984 and 1985, a period of explosive growth for that church.

From 1985 to 2003, as an Air Force Chaplain, Lieutenant Colonel Smith served Christian congregations around the world, experiencing many special ministry moments: flying weekly for four years as a Chaplain with the B-52 and KC-135 crews; skydiving with the Air Force Academy Collegiate Skydiving Team on a Sunday morning just prior to preaching a sermon entitled "Ponderings of a Plummeting Preacher"; teaching as a faculty member at the Air Force University for three years; serving as campus minister for 30,000 Keesler Air Force Base students and last but not least for Gary, representing the Air Force at the historic 1999 All-Star game with his then teenage daughter, Amity, at Boston's Fenway Park baseball stadium.

In 1991, Gary graduated first in a class of 604 officers in an Air Force leadership development school (Squadron Officer's School). In 1993 and 1995, Abington Press published Gary's sermons as a devotional series, receiving the highest positive feedback on record from readers around the country. Colonel Smith was also a speech writer for the Air Force Chief of Chaplains and for the current U.S. Deputy Secretary of Commerce, Dr. David Sampson.

After 31 years of service to his country (7 years enlisted, 5 years in the reserves, 19 years as a Chaplain), Colonel Smith retired in 2003, moving back to San Marcos, Texas where he lives with his wife Pamela and son Daniel. Daughter Amity and her husband Frank live in Auburn, Alabama.

For over twenty-six years, Gary has been inspired by the manner and styles of Dr. Michael Young, Dr. William Willimon and Dr. John Ed Mathison, three of the best Story tellers in ministry. As a minister working with Dr. Rod Coleman, Gary discovered his innate talents as a Story teller and in 1980 he adopted his current method of writing sermons by weaving God's Word into accounts of everyday life. Subscribers to his weekly e-Sermons embraced this refreshing approach and have finally encouraged Gary to release his first book, Letters from Boerdonk.

Gary presently serves as Senior Minister of a new church in San Marcos, Christ the Redeemer Church. The church, which has no denominational affiliation, is a place where people from diverse backgrounds gather to worship and celebrate the Love of Christ. Parishioners there enjoy Gary's message weekly as their hearts and minds are bonded through humor, tears and God's Word.

Watch for other Gary Layne Smith books in the near future.

Order Form
Letters from Boerdonk

Three ways to order copies of <u>Letters from Boerdonk</u>:

1) Online at http://www.HighPointPublishing.com
2) Call HighPoint Publishing, Inc at 1-512-858-2727
3) Copy this order form, fill it in and fax to 1-512-532-0783

Checks, Money Orders or bulk orders of more than ten books, please call.

Item	Quantity	Price Each	Total Price
Letters from Boerdonk ISBN-13: *978-1-933190-10-5*	*(max 10)*	$ 17.99	
Sales Tax *Texas residents only!*		$1.48 *per book* *8.25%*	
Shipping and Handling		**$4.95** *for one book* **$9.95** *for 2-10 books*	
Total Cost			

prices subject to change without notice

Name:

Address:

City: State: Zip Code:

Telephone:

Credit Card Number: CVV:

Expiration date: Email:

Orders placed by fax must be shipped to the credit card billing address.

HighPoint Publishing, Inc
141 Loop 64, Suite E
Dripping Springs, TX 78620
(512) 858-2727